PROFESSIONAL SKILLS FOR PSYCHOLOGY

Los Angeles | London | New Delhi
Singapore | Washington DC | Melbourne

Los Angeles | London | New Delhi
Singapore | Washington DC | Melbourne

SAGE Publications Ltd
1 Oliver's Yard
55 City Road
London EC1Y 1SP

SAGE Publications Inc.
2455 Teller Road
Thousand Oaks, California 91320

SAGE Publications India Pvt Ltd
B 1/I 1 Mohan Cooperative Industrial Area
Mathura Road
New Delhi 110 044

SAGE Publications Asia-Pacific Pte Ltd
3 Church Street
#10-04 Samsung Hub
Singapore 049483

Editor: Donna Goddard
Editorial assistant: Esmé Carter
Production editor: Imogen Roome
Copyeditor: Sarah Bury
Proofreader: Leigh Smithson
Indexer: Adam Pozner
Marketing manager: Fauzia Eastwood
Cover design: Wendy Scott
Typeset by: KnowledgeWorks Global Ltd.
Printed in the UK

**Library of Congress Control Number:
2021947977**

British Library Cataloguing in Publication data

A catalogue record for this book is available from the
British Library

ISBN 978-1-5264-8881-7
ISBN 978-1-5264-8880-0 (pbk)

At SAGE we take sustainability seriously. Most of our products are printed in the UK using responsibly
sourced papers and boards. When we print overseas we ensure sustainable papers are used as
measured by the PREPS grading system. We undertake an annual audit to monitor our sustainability.

Contents

About the Author

Judith Roberts is a HCPC-registered Clinical Psychologist with over 20 years' experience of working in Health and Social Care. She has her own private practice where she specialises in anxiety disorders and trauma. She is also Director of postgraduate studies and lecturer in the School of Human and Behavioural Sciences at Bangor University in North Wales, where she designed and delivers a Master's level module that teaches 'professional skills in psychology'. This book is borne from that module. Judith is a Senior Fellow at the Higher Education Academy (HEA) and she received a teaching fellowship from Bangor University in recognition of excellence in teaching and in supporting students in 2020.

Acknowledgements

I should like to thank my children, family, friends and colleagues, within and outside the NHS, who have contributed and supported my learning throughout my career. I will not name individuals, but those of you that have mentored and supervised me, and who have been there when all seemed too hard or celebrated my achievements, I could not have done this without you. I have also received a great deal of support from Esmé Carter, Donna Goddard, Marc Barnard, Katie Rabot and Robert Patterson, who have worked tirelessly in helping me put this book together.

Most importantly, I thank my faithful companion Jack, a dog who insists on his own needs being met when I've been in the throes of writing, which has helped me immeasurably by forcing much needed exercise and fresh air.

Introduction

This book represents my own experience of over 20 years of working in health and social care and in becoming and working as a Clinical Psychologist. It is an overview of what working as a practitioner psychologist entails from a contextual perspective. In addition to my practitioner role, I have worked in a university setting teaching and supporting students on undergraduate and postgraduate programmes for a number of years and have witnessed the challenges they face in deciding upon and pursuing a career as a practitioner psychologist. It can take years of study and endless searching for paid experience in the chosen field. It is therefore essential that, before embarking on such a journey, the student is fully aware that a career as a practitioner psychologist is not all about knowledge of mental health disorders, formulation, assessment and intervention. Having this knowledge and engaging in these activities may be the primary goal, but these are driven by a range of professional skills and knowledge, and it is competence in these professional skills and this knowledge, supported by practice experience, that can fully prepare the individual for practitioner psychology training, and beyond. Practitioner psychology roles are embedded in a range of settings, which include the NHS and community organisations. This book is not restricted to any particular setting but leans towards the professional skills and knowledge outlined as essential for NHS posts. It provides a concise overview of these professional skills and knowledge that are needed across a range of settings, and is a starting point for those who are considering a career as a practitioner psychologist.

Who is This Book for?

The intended audience for this book is first and foremost the student, whether undergraduate or postgraduate, and secondly, the educational setting/ programme developers. It has been designed to supplement a course of study, and includes learning outcomes and case study activities. I would also suggest that this text can aid with employability, as it outlines a range of skills and knowledge that the practitioner psychologist needs, and can underpin the focus on these skills as part of undergraduate and postgraduate psychology degrees. I have often found teaching professional skills challenging, as it is not considered as interesting as working therapeutically with service users, or learning about interventions for mental health disorders. It is always heartening, though, when I speak to a student who is working in the field or who has a place on a professional doctoral programme, when they reflect that, actually, the knowledge they gained from being taught professional skills has supported their practice in numerous ways.

I would also suggest that the chapters in this book can aid the practitioner when supervising assistant or trainee psychologists. It can take you back to basics, and can aid reflection on practice and what has been forgotten in the depths of organisational staleness, where change rarely occurs. The content can lead to new ideas, and therefore to new developments that can change the face of applying psychological theory and knowledge across different settings. It is not an exhaustive source of information, but a starting point.

Content Structure

The content of this book has been organised so as to illustrate the relationship between those skills that are organisational, those that are cultural in nature and those that are personal, that is, individual practitioner skills. Figure 0.1 visually organises each chapter into this overarching model, and a brief outline of each chapter is given below. The book can be 'dipped' into when required, so each chapter stands on its own, but together they provide an overview of the professional skills demanded from practitioner psychologists. Each chapter begins with a set of learning objectives before covering the content described below. Towards the end of the chapters there is a list of key points and two practice case studies with example questions that can be used to aid learning.

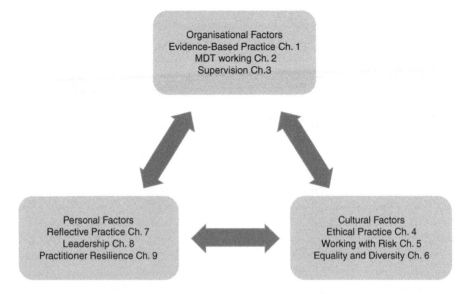

Figure 0.1   The professional context of practitioner psychologists: a three-factor model

Organisational Factors

Chapter 1. Evidence-Based Practice

Evidence-based practice (EBP) encompasses a three-stage approach that includes identifying and working with best evidence, utilising practitioner skills, and establishing service user values. At its core, it encapsulates the principle of working as a scientist-practitioner, which is the mainstay of training as a practitioner psychologist. The chapter provides an overview of each of the three elements of EBP. The section on best evidence describes randomised controlled trials, which are considered to be the 'gold standard' in research evidence, and considers efficacy of intervention versus effectiveness and what both of these terms mean. The chapter covers evidence-based databases and clinical guidelines, such as those produced by the National Institute for Health and Care Excellence (NICE). The section on clinical expertise covers the complexity of working with the human condition before moving to service user values and how a practitioner might identify those values. The chapter ends with an overview of empirically supported treatments and what fidelity in delivering those treatments means.

Chapter 2. Multidisciplinary Teams

A practitioner psychologist will more than likely work within a multidisciplinary team at some stage during their career. This chapter provides the reader with an overview of what a multidisciplinary team is and how it can support service user care. The chapter covers what an effective team might look like and how a team can be supported in facilitating and overcoming barriers to effective team working. Communication is highlighted, as well as the importance of team meetings and what the role of a practitioner psychologist is within those meetings. Conflict is discussed, as well as how to deal with conflict, and the importance of conflict in creating necessary change in organisational processes and culture. The chapter also covers relationship boundaries and power imbalances, both of which often contribute to conflict in teams.

Chapter 3. Supervision

The chapter on supervision begins with a definition of what clinical supervision is in comparison to other organisational types of supervision. The chapter focuses on three areas: (1) supervision and the service user, (2) supervision and the practitioner, and (3) supervision and the supervisor. It covers ethical principles and competence and how these serve the best interests of the service user. The chapter explores the supervisory contract and the skills required of an effective supervisor. As clinical supervision can encompass a range of different therapeutic modalities and supervision models, these are described.

Challenges in supervision are also discussed, and the chapter ends with a discussion on multicultural issues in clinical supervision.

Cultural Factors

Chapter 4. Ethical Practice

The chapter on ethical practice begin with an overview of professional codes of ethics and highlights the difference between regulations provided by the Health and Care Professions Council (HCPC) and British Psychological Society (BPS) guidelines. Ultimately, although there are principles to adhere to, there is no regulation or guideline that provides the practitioner with specific guidance on what to do in any given situation; this relies on practitioner skill and careful decision making. The chapter provides an overview of ethical issues such as boundaries, competence, confidentiality and informed consent, which includes coverage of capacity to consent. This chapter also covers research ethics and capacity to consent to research, and a brief overview of research ethics committees.

Chapter 5. Working with Risk

The chapter on working with risk begins with a definition of what risk is and what risk factors need to be considered in clinical practice. The principal themes covered in this chapter include risk assessment, risk assessment tools, risk of violence, risk of self-harm/suicide, risk of self-neglect, safeguarding, and risk management. The importance of a full multidisciplinary assessment of risk is examined, with a focus on placing the service user and their carer/family at the centre of this assessment. Good practice in risk assessment is discussed, with an overview of what difficulties can arise in risk assessment practices. The chapter looks at the actuarial systems and tools that are often used in risk assessment (this list is not exhaustive and is included to provide an insight into what these tools might look like). Practitioner safety is also discussed, particularly where violence or other risks may be present. Risk management is covered towards the end of the chapter with a brief overview of what positive risk management looks like in practice.

Chapter 6. Equality and Diversity

The chapter on equality and diversity begins with an outline of The Equality Act 2010, which aims to protect people against discrimination in employment and as consumers of public and private services. Both the legal perspective and the good practice perspective are considered. A model of anti-discriminatory practice for the practitioner psychologist is presented, which incorporates (1) interpersonal discrimination (including coverage of micro-aggressions), (2) organisational discrimination, and (3) societal discrimination. The chapter also covers what a culturally competent practitioner might look like, and how such a practitioner might challenge discrimination in day-to-day practice.

Personal Factors

Chapter 7. Reflective Practice

The chapter on reflective practice begins with an overview of its importance in clinical practice and its definition as a construct and as an activity. The chapter emphasises the messiness of human experience and how reflection is a deliberate form of thinking. Models of reflective practice are covered, which include Kolb's learning cycle (1984), Gibb's learning by doing model (1988), and Johns' reflective practitioner model (2000), with an emphasis that these are merely a lens with which to view reflection and not a specific recipe to follow. The chapter considers critical reflection and reflexivity before moving to the dark side of reflective practice and the potential for negative outcomes. The chapter also provides a list of skills that underpin critical reflective practice and ends with the practice of reflective writing and the importance of some form of feedback on our reflections, so as to aid learning and development.

Chapter 8. Leadership

The chapter on leadership considers what leadership skills look like for the practitioner psychologist. The chapter covers theories of leadership and how, over time, different skills have been seen as important in creating an effective leader. The nature of followers is also an important consideration because without support, leaders or those engaging in leadership roles will not progress towards their or their team's desired goals. As a key aspect of multidisciplinary working, leadership can be an organisational requirement as well as a personal endeavour, through the practice of self-leadership. Throughout the chapter a range of leadership skills are discussed and how these might translate into practice.

Chapter 9. Practitioner Resilience

The chapter on practitioner resilience considers how a drive to help people can often be rewarding, but can paradoxically push us beyond our limits, challenging our very core. The chapter covers areas of challenge, presenting some of the realities of practice, such as the experience of compassion fatigue, vicarious trauma and burnout. The chapter considers practitioner mental health and the impact of working with people who have mental health disorders, as well as self-disclosure and how this challenges boundaries. The chapter ends with consideration of self-care and what this looks like in practice. The aim of this chapter is to raise awareness of the impact of working with people and families in distress, and the importance of reflective practice and self-care practices in upholding the mental wellbeing of the practitioner.

Educational pathways to become a Practitioner Psychologist

Why did you choose to study psychology? It is an important question and one that I know I often reflect upon. You need to know the *why* before even contemplating the *how*. All sorts of psychological phenomena can capture our attention, whether it is a TV episode of Criminal Minds, a publicised study of behaviour, a personal or family event/illness, a natural disaster. It is all driven by human thought and behaviour. Although it can be challenging to pursue psychology as a career, as we all face our own psychological distress, we are still drawn in and fascinated by psychological phenomena. It might also be true that you chose psychology because you couldn't quite decide what to do, and only now have you decided that this is the career path for you.

> The following advice is designed to help you pursue your goal, to give you the best chance at attaining one of those places on postgraduate professional training programmes. Even when choosing your undergraduate psychology degree, it is important to choose a course that fits the accreditation requirements laid out by the British Psychological Society (BPS). It is also important to achieve the required grade so as to meet the entry requirements of professional/doctoral study. The following points need to be considered:

- Your undergraduate degree course (or postgraduate conversion course) needs to be accredited with the BPS. Accreditation means that the education provider (the university) has met the BPS quality standards in education and that the curriculum covers the minimum skills and knowledge required of a graduate in psychology. This means that upon graduating from a BPS-accredited course, the graduate has studied a sufficient breadth and depth of psychological theory to be able to progress to professional study in the field. Graduates who did not undertake their undergraduate degree in the UK can have their course of study recognised by the BPS through applying for graduate membership, but it is important to get in touch with the BPS for more information on what is or is not recognised. For graduates who did not study a BPS-accredited undergraduate degree, there are BPS-accredited Master's level conversion courses which meet accreditation standards. It is extremely important that the individual checks the accreditation status of their intended Master's degree course. A full list of conversion courses (and accredited undergraduate degrees) can be found at: www.bps.org.uk/public/become-psychologist.

- Completing a BPS-accredited undergraduate (or postgraduate conversion) degree provides you with 'Graduate Basis for Chartered Membership' (GBC), which is a requirement for BPS-accredited postgraduate and doctoral programmes, as well as for assistant psychology posts and some other positions that require previous study in psychology. The postgraduate training for the professions listed below all require GBC.
- As many of the practitioner psychologist training programmes (and assistant/trainee positions) are competitive, academic achievement at undergraduate degree level (or postgraduate conversion course) needs to be a high 2:1 or above. Applications for many clinical psychology doctoral courses are declined where the degree outcome is a 2:2 or below. Entry requirements do differ across practitioner psychologist training programmes though, so it is important that you check the programme website for accurate information.
- Over a three-year undergraduate degree, life happens, and this can derail our best efforts to perform to the best of our ability. University staff are there to help. There may be a pastoral care system, or student support service, that can give you the best advice with regard to taking time out, deferring a semester or repeating a year. It is better to give yourself the best chance at achieving the grades you need rather than struggling through and not quite making the grade for further postgraduate study.
- For practitioner psychologist training programmes that include a Master's as part of the training requirement (e.g. Health Psychologist, Forensic Psychologist), you must make sure that the Master of Science (MSc) programme you have chosen is accredited with the BPS for the career pathway you intend. Many Master's courses may have the term 'health psychology' or 'forensic psychology' in the title, but may not be accredited. Do contact the BPS or the course provider to check this if you are unsure.
- At the time of writing, applicants do not need a Master's degree to pursue the Doctorate in Clinical Psychology. This often leads to questions such as 'Will getting a Master's make it more likely that I get a training place?', or 'Will a Master's supercede an undergraduate degree that did not meet the 2:1 minimum requirement?'. Unfortunately, the answer to both questions is 'no'. Again, it is important that applicants check this before commencing (and paying for!) a Master's degree that they do not necessarily need. That said, the leap from undergraduate to doctoral study is significant, and a Master's can bridge the gap between academic ability and the skills and knowledge required to undertake doctoral study. In addition, studying a Master's degree requires students to be autonomous and self-motivated learners, which is a prerequisite for doctoral training. Another question that is often asked is 'Do I focus on getting clinical experience or pursuing

further study?'. I always advise students to pursue clinical experience in the first instance, as this can truly guide the individual in deciding whether they want to pursue psychology as their chosen profession. A second option is to undertake a part-time Master's degree alongside work experience, thus getting the best of both worlds.

- You can begin to gain relevant experience during your undergraduate degree through volunteering opportunities. These are often available via the student union or can be found through your university careers service. Although volunteering is not the same as paid clinical experience, it can be an important step towards securing paid clinical experience in the future. A few hours a week can make a big difference. Do be wary of 'voluntary' or 'honorary' assistant psychology positions where you are undertaking work that demands skills or knowledge that equates to what should be paid work. The lure of the 'assistant psychology' title can be strong in such a competitive field, but you must be discriminate in pursuing these opportunities. While honorary positions can often provide good, relevant experience, you need to ensure that you are given the support you need in carrying out your duties. Also remember that it is the activities of the post that will provide you with the skills and knowledge you need, not the job title. A support worker role can sometimes be a far richer experience than a role that has the title 'assistant psychologist'.

Practitioner Psychology Careers

The following list of professions shows the variety of career choices open to psychology graduates. For each profession, there is a brief outline of what it entails and details of the training required in order to pursue these careers following graduation from a BPS-accredited undergraduate degree or post-graduate conversion course in psychology. Do be aware that the application process for many programmes can take up to 12 months, so always check programme information.

Clinical Psychologist

Clinical Psychologists assess and deliver evidence-based interventions for a range of mental health conditions across the lifespan. They work with a range of people and groups, including those with brain injury, stroke, learning disabilities and dementia. They are trained as scientist-practitioners and are educated to doctoral level, through BPS-accredited postgraduate doctoral courses funded by the NHS. Clinical Psychologists work independently or as part of multidisciplinary teams. In addition to direct service user care, they are involved in service development and audit. Practitioners must be registered with the Health and Care Professions Council (HCPC) to use the title and to practise as Clinical Psychologists. For more information on the application process and funding for UK programmes see: www.leeds.ac.uk/chpccp/.

Counselling Psychologist

Counselling Psychologists use evidence-based psychological therapies to help people to cope with difficult life events and manage mental health disorders. In this role, practitioners work collaboratively with service users to encourage change and enable recovery. Much of the role is similar to that of Clinical Psychologists, and you will often see advertised posts asking for one or the other profession. To qualify as a Counselling Psychologist, candidates must undertake a BPS-accredited postgraduate doctoral degree in counselling psychology. Practitioners must be registered with the Health and Care Professions Council (HCPC) to use the title and to practise as Counselling Psychologists. Applications are made to individual programmes and a list of these can be found on the BPS website at: www.bps.org.uk/public/become-psychologist/accredited-courses.

Health Psychologist

Health Psychologists work with patients across the lifespan who are experiencing a range of physical or psychological health issues. Health Psychologists promote general wellbeing and healthy lifestyles as well as helping patients to understand their health issues and adjust to serious illness, such as cancer, and to use their expertise in diabetes management, pain management, needle phobia, and so on. Health Psychologists also work closely with other health professionals as well as with the families of patients. Assessment involves identifying behaviours that may damage health, the psychological impact of illness, and identifying appropriate evidence-based interventions. To become a Health Psychologist, you need to train at postgraduate level. There are two stages to qualifying as a Health Psychologist: stage 1 is completing a BPS-accredited MSc in health psychology, and stage 2 is either completing a BPS qualification in health psychology (QHP Stage 2), which is a doctoral-level qualification, or completing a BPS doctorate in health psychology (www.bps.org.uk/public/become-psychologist/accredited-courses). Health Psychologists need to be registered with the Health and Care Professions Council (HCPC) to use the title and practise as Health Psychologists.

Forensic Psychologist

Forensic Psychologists assess and treat perpetrators of crime as well as the victims of crime. They work with prisoners, offenders and other professionals, such as probation officers, and are required to give evidence in court and advise parole boards and mental health tribunals. They are heavily involved in risk assessment and rehabilitation. To become a Forensic Psychologist you need to train at postgraduate level. There are two stages to qualifying as a Forensic Psychologist: stage 1 is completing a BPS-accredited MSc in forensic psychology, and stage 2 is completing a BPS doctoral-level qualification in forensic psychology (QFP Stage 2). There are universities that offer the BPS Doctorate in Forensic Psychology (www.bps.org.uk/public/become-psychologist/accredited-courses), which negates the need to do both the MSc and BPS stage 2 course. Practitioners must be registered with the Health and Care Professions Council (HCPC) to use the title and practise as Forensic Psychologists.

Educational Psychologist

Educational Psychologists work with children and young people and apply psychological theory to problems related to successful learning and the engagement with school and other activities. Practitioners work collaboratively with teachers, social workers and parents. There is a great deal of focus on behaviour management and the delivery of learning programmes as well as offering consultation and training to teachers and teaching assistants. To train as an Educational Psychologist, the practitioner must attain a BPS Doctorate in Educational Psychology. The BPS lists courses for a BPS Doctorate in Educational Psychology (www.bps.org.uk/public/become-psychologist/accredited-courses). Information on how to apply will be available on each programme's university webpage. Practitioners must be registered with the Health and Care Professions Council (HCPC) in order to use the title and practise as Educational Psychologists.

Neuropsychologist

Neuropsychologists work with a range of individuals who have experienced traumatic brain injury, strokes and neurodegenerative diseases, such as dementia. Practitioners must have a significant degree of specialist knowledge in neuroscience in addition to knowledge of mental health disorders and the general skills and knowledge required by Clinical or Educational Psychologists. This is a 'post-doctoral' discipline, which means that to qualify as a Clinical Neuropsychologist the practitioner must first be either a qualified Clinical or Educational Psychologist. A distinction must be drawn here between academic neuropsychology and clinical neuropsychology. Academic neuropsychology focuses on the scientific understanding of neuropsychological function, whereas clinical neuropsychology is the application of that knowledge in clinical settings. The Qualification in Clinical Neuropsychology (QiCN) is a standard of competence that allows practitioners to demonstrate their knowledge and skills in this area. It is a BPS qualification that is studied as part of day-to-day clinical practice in a relevant setting where there is access to a neuropsychology caseload (e.g. brain injury services). Educational Psychologists pursue the pediatric pathway. On completion of this qualification, practitioners become full members of the Division of Neuropsychology (DoN) and are entered onto the BPS specialist register of Clinical Neuropsychologists.

Occupational Psychologist

Occupational Psychologists are based within employment/work settings and apply psychological theory to a range of individual and organisational issues, with aims such as increasing job satisfaction, improving productivity, cultivating team dynamics and developing corporate culture. Occupational Psychologists collaborate with management and human resource departments within the organisation. They can also work on a consultancy basis. The role includes engaging in counselling with individuals, assessing the design and functionality of work environments, and in recruitment, training and employee motivation. To qualify as an Occupational Psychologist, applicants must complete a BPS-accredited Master's course in Occupational Psychology, which typically takes one year full time and two years part time. Practitioners must then achieve the BPS Qualification in Occupational Psychology (QOP) Stage 2, which is approved by the Health and Care Professions Council (HCPC). The BPS QOP (Stage 2) is a doctoral-level programme consisting of two years of full-time (or the part-time equivalent) supervised practice. Practitioners need to be employed as trainee Occupational Psychologists. Once the BPS QOP is complete, practitioners can become registered with the HCPC and can use the title 'Occupational Psychologist'.

Sports Psychologists

Sports Psychologists are involved with sports and exercise, focusing on the behaviours and motivation of individuals, teams and organisations involved with either sport or exercise. Sports Psychologists work with amateurs as well as elite athletes, aiming to support the individual with their personal development and performance, and in facing the psychological demands of the sport. To qualify as a Sports Psychologist, the candidate must first complete a BPS-accredited MSc in Sport and Exercise Psychology before undertaking Stage 2 of the BPS Qualification in Sport and Exercise Psychology (QSEP), which involves two years of supervised practice. Practitioners can then register with the Health and Care Professions Council (HCPC) and can use the title 'Sport and Exercise Psychologist'. There are a small number of universities that have accredited doctoral programmes that lead to HCPC registration. You can search for HCPC-approved programmes at: www.hcpc-uk.org/education/approved-programmes/.

xx   **Professional Skills for Psychology**

Psychotherapist/Counsellors

Psychotherapists help service users to overcome a range of issues, including anxiety, depression, sleep disorders, work difficulties, addiction and relationship difficulties. Through engaging in therapeutic sessions, where the psychotherapist and service user discuss thought processes, feelings and behaviours, service users better understand their distress and can change the way they think and behave. There are a range of therapeutic models that psychotherapists can train in, including family and systemic therapies, psychodynamic therapy, psychoanalysis and behavioural therapy. For more information on psychotherapy, training courses as well as the nature of psychotherapy, the UK Council for Psychotherapy (UKCP; www.psychotherapy.org.uk/psychotherapy-training/train-as-a-psychotherapist/) is a useful source of information. The UKCP also accredits a number of training courses. Courses are also accredited by the British Association for Counselling and Psychotherapy (BACP; www.bacp.co.uk/search/Courses) and it is important to note that many of these courses are referred to as qualifications in counselling. Although there is no registration requirement for psychotherapists or counsellors, it is considered best practice to undertake a UKCP- or BACP-accredited course so that the practitioner can be voluntarily registered. This shows prospective service users and employers that the practitioner has a certain standard of education and training.

Work Experience

All the practitioner training programmes/courses listed here require a minimum level of appropriate work experience prior to application. My advice is to explore opportunities with private or public organisations where there is the potential for significant interaction with people who face health or psychological difficulties. This can include care work, support work, healthcare work, work as a teaching assistant, and working as a psychological wellbeing practitioner (PWP), although PWP work is a career in itself (see www.prospects.ac.uk/job-profiles/psychological-wellbeing-practitioner). It might be necessary to work voluntarily in the first instance, but of course this is often a barrier if it is not financially viable. It is also true that for some programmes of study (e.g. a Doctorate in Clinical Psychology), it is paid experience that is required, although voluntary work experience is sometimes needed in order to gain paid work experience.

Job roles such as those listed above can be advertised via organisation websites, NHS jobs, local authority websites (e.g. school assistant roles), community groups, etc. I also advise students to contact organisations directly; sometimes roles aren't advertised immediately or at all. If you find a role that you are interested in, be organised and be quick. Adverts for assistant psychology posts can sometimes be removed before the closing date due to the number of applications received. Do access the employability or careers service provided by your university as it can help with general advice on local organisations and opportunities, writing your CV, interviews, and so on.

The application form

Completing the application form is fairly straightforward. There are usually guides for applicants that can help you. It is imperative to follow such guides to the letter, so do make sure you read them. I would also advise that you get someone else to look over your application for any spelling or grammatical mistakes. You may have the most fantastic experience or academic grades, but a poorly put together application form will not lead to an interview.

Personal statements

Always make sure that your personal statement is specific to the job you apply for, and don't focus on the skills you don't have but highlight those that you do possess. Even if you feel you have little experience to reflect upon, you need to be able to recognise and communicate your own strengths, knowledge and motivation for pursuing the role. It is not about making yourself sound better than you are, but rather about recognising who you are and what you have to offer. When engaging in this type of reflection, don't just describe the skills you have achieved, reflect upon how you have achieved those skills. For example, if you want to say that you are excellent at communicating with a range of individuals, tell the reader how you have developed this skill (what is the evidence for this?) and in what way such a skill is useful for the role that you are applying for. Keep referring back to the specification for the job, using subheadings if this helps you to be clear, and place yourself in the position of the person recruiting for the job. A trap that is easy to fall into is to not fully explain your thinking, in other words, expecting the reader to fill in the gaps of what you mean in what you have written. For example, you assume the reader will know that you must be an excellent team player because you've said in your personal statement that you've been part of a team in a previous job role. Tell the reader why this makes you an excellent team player.

An often-neglected source of information for students who feel they have little in the way of practical work experience is that of the learning outcomes associated with each taught module. It can sometimes be surprising to real-ise that during that 12-week module on child development, you not only developed knowledge of child development, but also acquired expertise in public speaking (if you had an oral assessment), in working in a team (if there was group work), in being able to critically evaluate research literature (when completing an essay), in being able to manage your time (assessment dead-lines), in showing initiative and personal responsibility, in making decisions, in communicating information/ideas/arguments, and so on. Of course, a degree course can never replace real-world experience, but in being able to recognise and articulate the skills you have achieved during your degree, you are not only placing value on the skills that you have developed, you are also increasing your own confidence in what you have and can achieve.

Personal disclosure

Among those of us who have pursued a career as a practitioner psychologist, many have personal experiences that have led us to this career choice. For a student who is at the outset of this journey, it can sometimes be challenging to know what is and what is not appropriate information to share with potential employers or education providers. Share what you are comfortable sharing, whether this is in your personal statement or at the interview stage. The purpose of the personal statement and interview is for you to demonstrate whether you have the necessary skills for the position you have applied for, so do consider how you might demonstrate how your personal experience relates to this.

Referees

It is good practice to ask your previous/current employer or the academic staff at your place of study whether they are willing to provide you with a reference. You can indicate on application forms whether or not you want referees contacted before interview, but this does not mean that you should not let referees know of your intention. It is also useful for you to tell referees why you have chosen them to provide a reference, i.e. what they know about you, and what skills you feel they can best advise your potential future employer about. Don't just ask the people who you think like you!

Interviews

If you have secured an interview for a role, you have already shown that you have communicated your skills and experience to an excellent standard. Interviews are daunting. No matter where you are in your career, your age or your experience, interviews are challenging. Preparation is key, but there is a balance between being ready and being over-prepared. Rather than try to second-guess what the interview questions will be, think about what you have to offer the employer. What are your strengths and weaknesses? Think of examples where you have dealt with a difficult situation and learnt from it. What are you good at? Can you give an example to illustrate this? Hints and tips that can be useful are as follows:

- You are not expected to know everything. It is OK to say that you are not sure of something, but that you would be happy to receive the necessary training or to ask for advice.
- Pause, and breathe. Slow down. Show that you think things through before rushing in with an answer.
- Think of the interview as an opportunity to know more about the role, the organisation, and what they have to offer you in terms of training and opportunity (sometimes this can make the situation feel less daunting).
- The anxiety you feel during a stressful experience (such as a job interview) can either make you freeze or provide you with the acuity you need in order to share who you are and what you have to offer. If you go blank, breathe slowly and deeply, as this can allow your body's natural state of anxiety to calm down. If you need the panel to repeat a question, then ask them to do this (even if you don't need to, it can give a moment of breathing space).
- Remember – whether or not you get the job can sometimes be because you are one of many excellent applicants and the deciding factor may be something negligible. Do ask for feedback, though, as this can help inform future interviews.

Summary

This introduction has outlined the rationale for the book and the intended audience, who in the main are psychology students. My aim in this part of the book is to provide guidance on how to get to the career you want, to cover the basics of what a career in psychology could look like, and to advise on pursuing that goal. Some of the advice may not suit a mature applicant, who might already have a wealth of work experience in a particular health and social care setting, having long since completed a degree. That said, I feel it is useful to outline the landscape as it is for the majority of applicants who wish to pursue their career goal as quickly as possible (it is a long drawn-out process!). It is also true that even with that wealth of experience, the mature applicant may feel unsure about how to best present those skills and what they should focus on.

1

Evidence-Based Practice

On reading this chapter you will:

- Understand the scientist-practitioner model of training and practice
- Understand the three elements of the evidence-based practice (EBP) model
- Appreciate the complexity of identifying sources of 'best evidence' and understand the importance of adopting a critical stance when doing so
- Be able to reflect on your own clinical skills and identify areas of strengths and weaknesses
- Appreciate the importance of collaborating with the service user in identifying values
- Understand the concepts of efficacy versus effectiveness of therapeutic interventions
- Understand empirically supported treatments and the importance of fidelity

Introduction

With roots in evidence-based medicine, evidence-based practice evolved to encompass not only the use of current best evidence to make decisions about the care of patients in healthcare settings, but to acknowledge the skill level of the practitioner and the values of the service user so as to ensure the most appropriate intervention. It is an approach that must always guide the practitioner as opposed to being a stand-alone decision-making tool; the continuous assessment and formulation practice of the practitioner psychologist means that they are always checking in with their own skillset and in the appropriateness of the intervention based on service user characteristics and values. When choosing a particular therapeutic intervention or modality, there must be confidence in its safety and outcomes, and care in its application, consistent with the evidence base. This chapter will allow the reader to consider the challenges of working within the evidence-based practice model and to appreciate the strengths of the model in ensuring best practice.

Scientist-Practitioner Model

A chapter on evidence-based practice cannot proceed without placing it in the context of the training and the role of practitioner psychologists. Jones and Mehr (2007) outline the scientist-practitioner model (SPM) and offer an informative and accessible account of the foundations and practice of the SPM. In brief, they describe the SPM as a training model based on the ideology that practitioner psychologists should be trained in both research and clinical practice. According to Jones and Mehr, the SPM is based on the following assumptions:

- The SPM will facilitate effective psychological services.
- Continued research in the field adds to the development of scientific databases.
- By adopting a critical research approach in clinical practice, important social issues will come to the fore (making research in the field more relevant).

The term 'scientist-practitioner' was first introduced in 1949 at a conference on graduate training in psychology in Boulder, Colorado. Sometimes referred to as the 'Boulder model', the SPM has been adopted widely by practitioner psychology training programmes throughout Western countries. However, the model is not without its critics, with questions being raised as to whether practitioner psychologists, despite being trained in accordance with the SPM, combine the roles of researcher and practitioner when qualified, and whether this is actually necessary (Long & Hollin, 1997). According to Frank (1984, as cited in Long & Hollin, 1997), two dominant areas of contention are (1) that the skills and abilities needed in order to be a researcher are incompatible with those required of clinical practice, and therefore it is impossible to combine the two roles, and (2) that research training is unnecessary for practitioner psychologists. Frank asserts that in order to evidence the added value of the research training of practitioner psychologists, we must look at research output. Although such research (e.g. Norcross & Karpiak, 2012) suggests that the modal number of published articles authored by Clinical Psychologists is zero, Norcross and Karpiak also show that across 588 Clinical Psychologists surveyed in 2010, 47% were involved in research/writing activities. If this sample is representative of practitioner psychologists in general, it can be said that there are a number of practitioners involved in research activity. Not all research activity leads to publication, and relying on published research output may not be the best approach to measuring the impact and value of research training.

There are also other areas of clinical practice that benefit from research training (Jones & Mehr, 2007), namely:

- The recognition of the importance of using empirically supported treatments and the skills to evaluate those interventions.

- The consumption (understanding) of research can be incorporated into clinical practice.
- The ability to constantly evaluate service user progress in relation to intervention success.

Ultimately, the benefits of research skills and knowledge arguably enhance clinical practice. The avoidance of training in research and practice risks the abandonment of curiosity – the whys and hows of psychology practice. Discussion of the SPM leads the chapter nicely into the main focus, which is evidence-based practice. Evidence-based practice embodies the qualities of the SPM training approach by focusing on evidence, evaluation and practice.

An Introduction to Evidence-Based Practice

Evidence-based practice (EBP) informs the process of clinical decision making in health care. The earliest definition by Sackett, Rosenberg, Gray, Haynes and Richardson (1996: 3) states that EBP is 'the conscientious, explicit, judicious use of current best evidence in making decisions about the care of individual patients' (see also Sackett, 1997). This early definition adopted in medicine has since been adapted to suit other healthcare professions, such as nursing (Craig & Smyth, 2002) and social work (Gibbs, 2002). The American Psychological Association (APA) defined the EBP model for psychology as follows:

> Evidence-based practice in psychology is the integration of the best available research with clinical expertise in the context of patient characteristics, culture and preferences. (APA Presidential Task Force on Evidence-Based Practice, 2006: 273)

While the APA proposed the model of EBP in psychology, they did not clearly lay out the skills required for EBP. Spring (2007) proposed 'the three-legged stool' as a metaphor for EBP, encompassing the three basic elements of EBP: best evidence, clinical expertise and service user values. This tangible addition to the literature on EBP in psychology offers a firm foundation on which to identify the core skills and competencies required when engaging in EPB. Figure 1.1 illustrates the basic elements of the model.

Misconceptions about EBP

Before describing the three legs of the EBP stool in greater depth, it is necessary to dispel any assumption or confusion about what EBP is and, in particular, what it is not. When exploring the research literature on the topic, the term 'evidence-based practice' can be interchanged with 'empirically supported treatments', i.e. therapeutic approaches that have been shown to be effective/ efficacious. EBP can also be used to mean the use of clinical guidelines. This

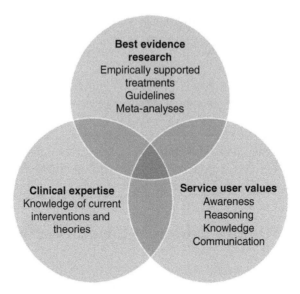

Figure 1.1   A model of evidence-based practice

may be as a result of the earlier medical definition proposed for EBP. In this chapter, EBP is used in Figure 1.1 to describe the elements mentioned by Spring (2007).

Best Evidence

Although seemingly straightforward, the decision as to what constitutes 'best evidence' is challenging, particularly for the busy practitioner psychologist. If we need to justify our approach to treatment, then it is prudent to adopt a method or intervention that has been shown in research trials to work for the majority of people. The 'hierarchy of evidence' stems from the medical literature and lists sources of research evidence in order of quality (see Guyatt et al., 1995). Additionally, the 'hierarchy of evidence' stipulates that the 'best evidence' comes from research methods such as the randomised controlled trial (RCT), which is least subject to bias or error, or systematic reviews/ meta-analyses, which are based on RCTs. Within the 'hierarchy of evidence' there is a distinction between (1) research that demonstrates efficacy, where the therapeutic approaches are shown to be effective in tightly controlled experimental settings, and (2) research that demonstrates effectiveness, where therapeutic approaches are shown to be effective within the uncontrolled clinical setting (see Seligman, 1995). Regardless of debates surrounding what is and what is not a valuable scientific approach in psychology, the fact remains that psychologists are resistant to relying on scientific literature due to its focus on objectivity, which is far removed from the subjective nature of therapeutic intervention (Lilienfeld, Ritschel, Lynn, Cautin, & Latzman, 2013). This gap of ideals hinders any progress in EBP, which at its core lies in a need to do the best for our service users through delivering effective therapies.

What is considered 'best evidence'?

As previously noted, 'best evidence' is typically illustrated by the 'hierarchy of evidence'. The RCT is considered the 'gold standard' in assessing treatment efficacy but is not the only methodological approach that can assess the effectiveness of therapeutic interventions. Meta-analysis is considered the optimal summary of evidence as it brings together RCTs in a quantitative review. The hierarchy of evidence, as defined by Guyatt et al. (1995) and listed in order of 'best evidence', is (1) systematic reviews and meta-analysis, (2) RCTs with definitive results, (3) RCTs with non-definitive results, (4) cohort studies, (5) case control studies, (6) cross-sectional studies, and (7) case reports. The noted absence in this list is qualitative research, where the focus is on interpreting experience and on understanding the individual's perspective. This is because, from a medical standpoint, interventions are aimed at finding a cure through objective data-driven approaches rather than focusing on an individual's experience of a condition (although arguably this is changing). Despite the move to adopt EBP within psychology, much of the literature remains rooted in medicine. This impacts on how research in psychology is conducted, with funding and dissemination guided by the traditional view of 'best evidence'.

Randomised controlled trials in psychology

The RCT consists of two or more groups of participants who are randomly allocated (to avoid bias) into a treatment group or groups and a control group or groups so that treatment effects can be isolated. Optimally, the researcher and the participant are unaware of which group they are in (known as a double-blind study), or if this is not possible, it may require a single-blind process (where either the researcher or the participant is unaware of what group they are in) or no blinding at all. When looking at therapeutic methods and interventions, it is impossible to 'blind' the researcher as they will be trained in whichever treatment modality is under scrutiny and will therefore know what is being delivered. Equally, the participant may well realise which treatment they are receiving, having being informed of the study aims. RCTs are therefore, arguably, better suited to experiments involving pharmacological products or medical procedures. A placebo pill is easy enough to administer, whereas a 'treatment as usual' approach in therapeutic research is difficult to operationalise given the variation in typical clinical work.

Efficacy versus effectiveness

A frequent debate when considering the quality of the evidence base of a particular psychological treatment is whether the clinician should place priority on research that demonstrates *efficacy* or research that shows that a particular intervention is *effective*. It can be a challenge to remember the distinction between the two, but it is an essential consideration when attempting to translate success in research to good outcomes in clinical practice. In brief, *efficacy* refers to the internal validity of the study (that the results of the study are trustworthy) whereas *effectiveness* is about maximising the external validity (that the results of the study can be replicated in real-life settings) and balancing this with internal validity. Externally valid research is typically conducted in clinical settings that provide psychological services. Crucially, the balancing act between efficacy and effectiveness is a well-debated topic within the literature.

Evidence-based databases

Issues facing the busy practitioner when keeping up to date with the most relevant literature related to therapeutic methods and interventions comprise access and availability, time and cost. Practitioners can often resort to the use of tried-and-tested methods or a quick chat with colleagues on how to proceed with an individual service user. Practitioners can do an internet search of tools and resources applicable to whichever condition they are presented with (e.g. depression or anxiety) and therapeutic modality (e.g. cognitive behavioural therapy), but this does not constitute working within the boundaries of EBP. One approach might be to consult primary databases which house peer-reviewed primary research (studies that have collected data that has not been gathered before and that has been reviewed by experts in the field prior to publication).

When using primary databases, it is up to the practitioner to evaluate the scientific rigour and validity of the data and to incorporate the results into a clinically valid approach (over and above the peer review process). The most popular primary databases are PsychINFO, which, as its name suggests, comprises psychological and psychiatric journals, MEDLINE and CINAHL, which contain a vast array of research articles that can provide fruitful results when exploring a particular clinical question (Falzon, Davidson, & Bruns, 2010). However, a key issue facing practitioners is the ever-changing world of health-related research, and therefore keeping up to date with recent advances in the field can be challenging. When looking at the time it would take to read all the published material relevant to their practice, Alper et al. (2004) estimated 627.5 hours. This is therefore not the most time-efficient or even achievable approach to take.

Evidence-based databases are distinct from primary databases. Evidence-based databases summarise primary research through systematic reviews. Arguably the most popular evidence-based database is produced by *Cochrane* (previously known as the Cochrane Collaboration). Cochrane produce systematic reviews specifically related to health (including psychological health) and are designed to be used by health practitioners. Cochrane UK is funded by the National Institute of Health Research (NIHR), which supports the development of Cochrane systematic reviews through a learning and development programme. Cochrane systematic reviews are housed in the Cochrane database of systematic reviews (www.cochrane.org/). Most importantly, abstracts of the reviews are available free of charge. Cochrane reviews also inform the development of National Institute of Clinical Excellence (NICE) and the Scottish Intercollegiate Guidelines Network (SIGN) guidelines. Importantly, the Cochrane evidence-based database removes the need for the busy practitioner to review primary research evidence. It should be noted, though, that the rigour applied to Cochrane systematic reviews may exclude some of the more niche topics or experiential approaches (e.g. qualitative research).

NICE guidelines

Clinical guidelines are now prolific in providing the evidence base in an accessible form for the busy clinician within physical and psychological service provision (Parry, Cape, & Pilling, 2003). Clinical guidelines are based on a review of the research literature that is considered by a committee made up of practitioners, care providers, commissioners, service users and carers. One of the most well-known providers of clinical guidelines is the National Institute of Health and Social Care Excellence (NICE), which aims to improve health and social care by (1) producing evidence-based guidance and advice, (2) developing quality standards and performance metrics for providers and commissioners of services, and (3) providing information services for commissioners, practitioners and managers. NICE provides guidance for the National Health Service (NHS), local authorities, employers, voluntary groups and any other groups that deliver health and social care services. The website (www.nice.org.uk/) is accessible to the general public, illustrating the organisation's aims of openness and accessibility.

NICE was set up in 1999 to reduce variation in treatments and care provision across the NHS (it was initially named 'National Institute for Clinical Excellence). Through a merger with the Health Development Agency in 2005, public health guidance was produced and the name was changed to 'National Institute for *Health* and Clinical Excellence'. In 2013 NICE became rooted in primary legislation and became a statutory body, as outlined in the Health and Social Care Act 2012. The name was changed again to 'National Institute for Health and *Care* Excellence' to accommodate these developments. Importantly, due to the way NICE was established in legislation, the guidance is only official in England. Products are available to Wales, Scotland and Northern Ireland through special agreements. Ultimately, guidelines developed by NICE are the 'go to' database for the busy practitioner.

Although the aims of guidelines, such as those produced by NICE, are to encourage practitioners to engage in practice that is supported by the evidence, making such evidence relevant and practice-focused, there are potential problems and limitations in how guidelines are produced. As noted by Woolf, Grol, Hutchinson, Eccles and Grimshaw (1999), it is foolhardy to assume that the recommendations made in guidelines are without error. Members of the guideline group are typically the very professionals who would use the guidelines in their practice, so it is ironic that those members are under the same time, resource and skills limitations as their colleagues, leading to unintentional oversights and errors in their analysis. Woolf and colleagues highlight three areas where such oversights or errors occur: (1) there is a lack of good quality, well-designed research evidence, (2) guideline development groups are limited by the opinions and experience of the members, who may hold misconceptions as to what works, and (3) the needs of the service user may be overridden by costs, societal needs or special interests (e.g. political agendas). If guidelines are adhered to blindly, interventions or approaches that are ineffective, and at the very worst harmful, can become the norm. In contrast, Court, Cooke and Scrivener (2017) highlight the barriers to implementing and adhering to such guidelines, and provide an interesting overview of the reasons why practitioner psychologists may not routinely use guidelines. It seems that evidence-based guidelines, despite their aims, are not without problems, and within the context of EBP they may not serve their intended purpose.

Clinical Expertise

Much of the training in most healthcare professions utilises a competency-based framework where practice experiences inform certain skill requirements, such as communication, alliance building, etc. For practitioner psychologists, assessment and formulation skills are a core requirement, in addition to being competent in evaluating and delivering empirically supported treatments. While easy to monitor and assess throughout training, once qualified, clinical expertise is assumed to grow throughout the career, with importance being placed on continuing professional development and recognition of competency gaps through reflection and clinical supervision. However, the measurement and explicit recognition of clinical expertise as a component of EBP is weak, and possibly absent in some cases (Spring, 2007; Lilienfeld et al., 2013).

Lilienfeld et al. (2013) state that clinical expertise is made up of both clinical judgement and clinical experience. Although experience is measurable in time or qualifications, good judgement is not necessarily an outcome of lengthy experience. Bourne, Kole, Healy, Hambrick and Wai (2014) suggest that the term 'expertise' implies being the best at what you do – being an 'expert' whose performance is superior. Such a label is heavy with expectancy, in that the practitioner may expect that in order to engage in EBP they need this 'expertise', and be reluctant to be defined by this label, given the power and status connotations inherent in the term. There is even some suggestion inherent in the term that being seen by an expert brings with it a better service. Bourne and colleagues further suggest that expertise is built through practice and experience, on a foundation of innate ability and talent. There is no doubt that this seems a fair explanation of expertise in a general sense. To qualify as a practitioner psychologist requires a battle through a lengthy recruitment process, leading to the development of clinical skill across a range of practice placements, in addition to academic tasks and research. Rather than view expertise as an end goal, where you have reached the pinnacle of your career, expertise would be better viewed as a process of 'being the best at what you can do'.

To place 'expertise' in context, we have to consider the reality of working as a practitioner psychologist engaging in psychotherapeutic work. Goodheart (2006) reminds us of the reality of what therapeutic work entails, and that 'expertise' is better understood as the ability to endure the messiness of human endeavour, rather than having years of experience and typically a wide range of academic texts on the shelf that are unused and unread.

Clinical expertise

Clinical expertise involves the following:

- The ability to 'sit with' the messiness of human experience.
- Strength of character, illustrated by persistence and acceptance of challenges.
- Acknowledging that 'knowledge' changes: expertise is the ability to negotiate the ever-changing face of psychology as a science and to accept that what we know today may not be that informative five years into the future.
- The ability to adopt an approach informed by multiple sources of information (rarely in human sciences is there an absolute answer for any one situation).

How does clinical expertise develop? A useful approach outlined by Petty (2015) is to learn from our experience by engaging in the following:

- Reflecting on and learning from our clinical experience.
- Adopting a questioning and critical approach to clinical experiences.

- Being open to change and adapting to new knowledge.
- Welcoming alternative views and perspectives.

Service User Values

Described as 'patient values' by Spring (2007), the term 'service user' is used here as a better representation of the psychological rather than medical approach. As its title suggests, and in line with the APA's definition of EBP, service user values, preferences and culture should inform the practitioner's use of the best available evidence, which will rely primarily on clinical expertise and the skills therein. Of course, the service user is unlikely to present with clearly laid out values and with the confidence to assert their right for partnership. Indeed, there may be an implicit expectation that the practitioner is the expert and there may be resistance in moving away from this paternalistic model. It is therefore the practitioner who should explicitly highlight the need for collaboration in choosing and engaging with the mode of therapy or intervention used. In doing so, the practitioner should ensure that the service user is aware of the risks and benefits of a range of therapeutic modalities, and includes recognition of the role of pharmacological approaches to treatment. One size does not fit all.

When deciding on the best treatment approach, regardless of the quality of evidence or the practitioner's experience, it is the expectations and hopes of the service user that determine the chosen approach. A tension exists between doing what is believed to be in the service user's best interest and what the client actually wants. It is arguably clinical expertise that overcomes this tension, but it is not without risks – specifically, the risk of disengagement and potentially the risk of harm. The potential for misuse of power in the therapeutic relationship influences these decisions, hence the ethical need for the consideration of service user values. It is not to be assumed, however, that values are equivalent to ethics (i.e. justice and best interests). Values incorporate what constitutes a life worth living for the service user, such as honesty, self-esteem, and a right to be heard.

The interpretative quality of values and their fluidity in changing over time leads to questions about having a consistent approach to incorporating values within EBP. There is no 'right' or 'wrong' in values (other than those rooted in the ethics of 'no harm'). We cannot create a list of values that must be adhered to as this would be unending and would perpetuate the idea that there is such a thing as values that are 'wrong'. Eliciting service user values is a subjective endeavour laden with bias. Therefore, some points to consider in engaging in this process (and an acceptance that eliciting service user values will never be a straightforward task) are outlined below. These were based on those developed by Woodbridge and Fulford (2004), whose workbook on values is a highly valuable resource for professionals working in health and social care.

Identifying service user values

Awareness: Identifying a service user's values is essential. However, it is not an easy task as asking the individual to identify their values may result in confusion (for the service user and practitioner!). A useful exercise in highlighting the difficulty in identifying values is to ask yourself what your values are. Much of the problem lies with the meaning underlying the word 'values'. It is necessary not only to explain what is meant by 'values' to the service user, but also to use our clinical skills to notice how the service user speaks about their life, their history, their friends and family, and so forth. A great deal of value-laden information can be elicited in this way. A further consideration is the values of the social system and the professional setting. Any mismatch in values within external systems can result in problems within the therapeutic setting. An approach of openness and partnership is therefore recommended. Asking someone about what is important to them without explaining why this information is important should be avoided. It should also be a continuous task – values are subjective and therefore change over time. Checking in with the service user and keeping an awareness of values throughout the therapeutic journey is essential.

Reasoning: Despite the fact that values are deemed to be subjective, are neither right nor wrong, and should be considered without judgement, values are subject to change and therefore they are open to discussion. To reason about values is to consider their meaning, their source and their impact. Not only do the service user's values require reasoning, but so do the practitioner's values. Through engaging in this practice, certain beliefs and attitudes may be identified which determine the success or lack of success of certain interventions and approaches. Ignoring service user values when adopting a particular intervention or approach can lead to negative consequences, such as non-engagement or non-compliance.

Knowledge: Inherent in EBP is the importance of knowledge. When considered in relation to values, it is about identifying gaps in knowledge about what is personally important (for both service user and practitioner) as well as ensuring that the service user is fully informed at every step. It is about providing the service user with the opportunity to assess information about how any particular intervention or approach may challenge or meet their particular needs.

Communication: The ability to communicate with a range of individuals is central to any profession that works with vulnerable populations. Over and above seeking shared knowledge of the objective facts of the situation, it is seeking a communication style that allows the sharing of values. This is where skills such as listening and empathy, adaptation of language to meet the skills of the service user, adaptation of environmental cues and an overt acceptance of multiple perspectives, leading to negotiation and conflict resolution, are essential.

Responding to values and treatment effectiveness

An important concern is treatment effectiveness and, in particular, how to adapt our therapeutic approach while responding to service user values. The clinician may be reluctant to administer a therapy or intervention that does not have the strongest evidence base (or adheres to strict guidelines such as those outlined by Cochrane). There are two important considerations here:

1. Even though an intervention may not have a robust evidence base, it may still be effective, particularly if it meets the service user's values. The clinician can explore alternatives through accessing evidence supported by research methodologies which may not meet the requirements of evidence-based databases and clinical guidelines (e.g. qualitative research).
2. When engaging in shared decision making about the best approach, it must be remembered that the service user will need unbiased information on what the alternative interventions are so that their decision is informed.

Evidence-Based Practice vs Empirically Supported Treatments

Empirically supported treatments (ESTs) are sometimes referred to as EBP when in fact they are different. However, ESTs can be used as part of an EBP approach. As the name suggests, ESTs are therapies and interventions that have an evidence base that supports their efficacy. A report on psychological interventions and a subsequent list of ESTs (initially termed 'empirically validated psychological treatments') were first published by the Task Force on Promotion and Dissemination of Psychological Procedures of Division 12 (Clinical Psychology) of the American Psychological Association (Task Force, 1995). Subsequent reports were added (Chambless et al., 1996; Chambless & Hollon, 1998) and these have been updated and debated in the literature ever since. According to Tolin, McKay, Forman, Klonsky, and Thombs (2015), despite the intent of such reports in ensuring evidenced treatments, the EST approach has been subject to a great deal of critique. This includes the absence of focus on negative findings, favouring statistical significance rather than clinical significance, inadequate focus on long-term outcomes, variable study quality, poor translation of empirical support into practice recommendations, consideration of the effectiveness in non-research settings, and an emphasis on specific diagnoses. Such criticisms can be overcome and their identification is a valuable first step. Tolin et al. propose that the criteria upon which to determine the quality of ESTs should be revised to include updated recommendations that overcome these problems.

Practitioner psychology training includes ESTs as a basis for clinical practice teaching. ESTs such as cognitive behavioural therapy (CBT) are well established and form the foundations of many training programmes. Having highlighted the potential problems with ESTs, the following recommendations for practice are made:

- Practitioners need to acknowledge the limits of research methods and adopt a critical approach to evidenced outcomes, recognising any inherent limitations.
- Having a clear approach to fidelity (see below) and knowledge of the core characteristics of a treatment helps practitioners to adapt that treatment to a variety of settings and service users.
- Do not dismiss ESTs based on prior negative experiences. Making appropriate adaptations to a treatment can be a challenge. Use peer knowledge and supervision to critique the approach and to reflect on what hasn't been effective and what has.

Fidelity in Delivering Empirically Supported Treatments

One of the persistent problems with delivering empirically supported treatments is whether they are delivered in the way that was intended, that is, the way that was shown to be effective when the research was conducted. Fidelity is therefore defined here as how closely the practitioner psychologist adheres to the intended delivery approach of the intervention they wish to use. The issue is that if the research supporting the intervention is based on a particular method of delivery, any change or adaptation of this method invalidates the evidence upon which it was based. Of course, if we consider the central elements of EBP, it is not only the evidence base that must be prioritised, but also the clinician's expertise and service user values. To deliver an intervention based solely on the evidence without any discretion not only contradicts the assumptions of the scientist-practitioner model (SPM), but also introduces the idea that if an intervention is manualised, why does it need to be delivered by a profession that demands years of costly training? What is the added value of a practitioner psychologist? The answer lies in the ability of the practitioner to adopt practices that support fidelity while flexibly adapting to external variables, which requires a great deal of skill.

It is generally accepted that practitioners make small changes to interventions that require some level of fidelity following training in that intervention.

Such changes can include adopting methods of delivery that are inconsistent with that suggested by the intervention protocol. According Stirman et al. (2015), modifications to ESTs can be defined as follows:

- Fidelity-consistent modifications – these do not alter the primary elements of an intervention or treatment so that adherence to the protocol is maintained.
- Fidelity-inconsistent modifications – these do alter the primary elements of an intervention or treatment so that adherence to the protocol is compromised.

Stirman and colleagues highlighted the importance of practitioner characteristics and how these lead to fidelity-consistent practices and fidelity-inconsistent practices. The authors examined such characteristics in practitioners (n = 27) who had received workshop training in cognitive behavioural therapy (CBT) for either child or adult populations who experienced symptoms of depression and anxiety. Within these workshops, fidelity was emphasised and defined as keeping to the core elements of the treatments. Participants were also encouraged to self-assess their fidelity after training. The primary outcome of this study was based on the openness and willingness of participants in adopting ESTs. Participating practitioners who were *open* to using ESTs (i.e. they were keen to adhere to the treatment protocol but recognised that some adaptation was necessary to make these work in clinical settings) tended to make fidelity-consistent modifications. Participating practitioners who found the treatment less appealing (i.e. they were less *willing* to adopt it) were shown to see less value in maintaining fidelity and tended to adopt fidelity-inconsistent practices. How can we overcome such issues? As outlined by Stirman et al. (2015), a focus on fidelity practices and outcomes could inform in-training approaches that incorporate discussion on acceptable adaptations that retain the integrity of the evidence base. Fidelity is therefore dependent on the practitioner's ability to balance what has been evidenced as effective in research against its delivery in practice.

Summary

Evidence-based practice as a process of decision making in health care ensures that interventions are fit for purpose. The combined focus on best evidence, clinical expertise and service user values offers a comprehensive starting point, and encourages a critical stance in how we conduct our work. That said, when you consider the challenges in determining what constitutes 'best evidence', the reliance on efficacy rather than effectiveness, the problematic nature of RCTs and EBDs, it is clear to see why practitioner psychologists are somewhat reluctant to fully embrace EBP. Although there are inherent problems with guidelines, such as those by NICE, they do serve as a valuable source of information and guidance. It is for the clinician to explore the foundations of such guidelines, to use their expertise in judging the usability of those guidelines and, at the very least, to become familiar with approaches that are recommended. Empirically supported treatments are supported by the evidence when delivered as intended. However, fidelity to such interventions has to be measured against the practicalities of the service user and the setting.

It is easy to become habituated to our working practices. We do what we know best. Expertise as a process requires deliberate action by the practitioner. Such action requires a concerted effort to make time to reflect in one-to-one supervision and peer-supervision. The latter is valuable as multiple perspectives and approaches can be shared. Although such time might be viewed as a luxury with ever-lengthening waiting lists and organisational demands, the practitioner psychologist is in a prime position to argue for such practices and to effect their inclusion in job plans. Ultimately, it is a professional requirement of governing bodies such as the Health and Care Professions Council (HCPC) that practitioner psychologists engage in continuing professional development, supervision and reflection so that they are competent in the service they provide to the service user, the team, the organisation and their own development.

Although the focus of service user values is primarily on the service user, other values should be considered as these feed into service user values. These include clinician and systemic values. Values change over time, and it is not a 'one time' check-in that is then noted in the service user's file, but is something that should form part of the therapeutic journey. Points to consider include awareness, reasoning, knowledge and communication. Identifying and responding to values can be a time-consuming endeavour, but is an essential component of EBP. It could be argued that 'evidence' encompasses not only the outcomes of research into treatment efficacy, but also how those outcomes measure up to the values and preferences of individual service users.

Working according to a particular practice model may sound straightforward but there are important considerations that need to be made. We must remind ourselves that working as a practitioner psychologist in health care is a process rather than a specific set of practices. That said, the EBP model represents key areas within the process of working with service users, and indeed working towards other key responsibilities, such as conducting research, teaching, service development and clinical supervision. Efficacy and effectiveness are key considerations as well as fidelity in delivery. With deliberate action and a critical stance, the practitioner can navigate the path of evidence-based practice with the understanding that we have to acknowledge that psychological interventions are rarely of a 'one size fits all' design.

Key Points

- The scientist-practitioner model asserts that practitioner psychologists should be trained in both research and practice.
- Evidence-based practice is the integration of 'best evidence', 'clinical expertise' and 'service user values'.
- Efficacy refers to the internal validity of a study whereas effectiveness relates to the external validity, i.e. research conducted in real-life settings.
- Evidence-based databases and clinical guidelines rely heavily on studies that demonstrate efficacy.
- Clinical expertise is a process of deliberate enquiry.
- Service user values can be identified with awareness, reasoning, knowledge and communication.

Practice Case Studies

Case Study 1

You are a Clinical Psychologist working in a child and adolescent mental health team. The team consists of a mix of professions and includes a psychiatrist, two other Clinical Psychologists and a cognitive behavioural therapist. You enjoy your work and this is your first job since qualifying. You have been with the team for 12 months.

You meet with your supervisor every two weeks. Your supervisor is a senior Clinical Psychologist based within your team. You feel supported but often worry that your supervisor tends to focus on managerial elements, such as your workload, weekly tasks and meetings and annual leave. You were hoping that you would be encouraged to seek further training in evidence-based approaches, such as dialectical behaviour therapy (DBT) or cognitive analytic therapy (CAT), both of which have been shown to be beneficial for adolescents who engage in self-harm and who have difficulties in developing healthy relationships.

As an early career Clinical Psychologist, you feel it is important to develop skills that will enhance your current work and to pursue opportunities for career progression. The lack of focus on training is an issue for the team as a whole and this frustrates you.

Suggested questions

1. Which aspects of this chapter can you use in your request for further training in DBT and CAT?
2. Who would you approach with this request?

Case Study 2

You have recently begun working with Katie (16 years old), who was referred into your team by her GP. The referral stated that Katie was low in mood, unmotivated and frequently absent from school. You have met with Katie twice. She comes to sessions alone, having been dropped off by a family member on both occasions. According to Katie, her goals for therapy are (1) to be more confident, and (2) to be able to make friends.

Katie is an only child and lives with her mum and dad. Both her parents work full time and Katie is often left alone. Her parents appear supportive and Katie does not report any difficulties at home. Katie is able to look after herself and presents as being mature for her age.

Katie is pleasant and attentive and appears to engage well. You have spent some time getting to know her and your initial formulation is that Katie is low in confidence and self-esteem, which impacts on her ability to make friends. You have shared this assessment with Katie and explained that you feel a cognitive behavioural therapy (CBT) approach would be best.

Katie, although polite, states in no uncertain terms that CBT is not for her. You gain the impression that if you were to pursue the issue, Katie would not attend your sessions. It transpires that Katie had heard her mum talk about 'CBT' to her aunt and the impression it gave Katie was that it involved a great deal of 'homework' and was 'less than useless'.

Suggested questions

1. Based on the information in this chapter, what would inform your next step?
2. Do you choose another therapy/intervention? Why?
3. How would you overcome the challenges that you might face should you continue with a CBT approach?

References

Alper, B. S., Hand, J. A., Elliott, S. G., Kinkade, S., Hauan, M. J., Onion, D. K., & Sklar, B. M. (2004). How much effort is needed to keep up with the literature relevant for primary care? *Journal of the Medical Library Association: JMLA*, 92(4), 429–437. Retrieved from www.ncbi.nlm.nih.gov/pubmed/15494758

APA Presidential Task Force on Evidence-Based Practice. (2006). Evidence-based practice in psychology. *American Psychologist*, 61(4), 271–285. https://doi.org/10.1037/0003-066X.61.4.271

Bourne, L. E., Kole, J. A., Healy, A. F., Hambrick, D. Z., & Wai, J. (2014). Expertise: Defined, described, explained. *Frontiers in Psychology*, 4 March. https://doi.org/10.3389/fpsyg.2014.00186

Chambless, D. L., & Hollon, S. D. (1998). Defining empirically supported therapies. *Journal of Consulting and Clinical Psychology*, 66(1), 7.

Chambless, D. L., Sanderson, W. C., Shoham, V., Johnson, S. B., Pope, K. S., Crits-Christoph, P., … McCurry, S. (1996). An update on empirically validated therapies. *The Clinical Psychologist, 49*(2), 5–18.

Court, A. J., Cooke, A., & Scrivener, A. (2017). They're NICE and neat, but are they useful? A grounded theory of clinical psychologists' beliefs about and use of NICE Guidelines. *Clinical Psychology & Psychotherapy, 24*(4), 899–910. https://doi.org/10.1002/cpp.2054

Craig, J. V., & Smyth, R. L. (Eds.). (2002). *The Evidence-Based Practice Manual for Nurses.* Edinburgh: Churchill Livingstone.

Department of Health (2012) *The Health and Social Care Act (2012).* London: HMSO. Available at https://www.legislation.gov.uk/ukpga/2012/7/contents (accessed: 2 February 2021).

Falzon, L., Davidson, K. W., & Bruns, D. (2010). Evidence searching for evidence-based psychology practice. *Professional Psychology: Research and Practice, 41*(6), 550–557. https://doi.org/10.1037/a0021352

Gibbs, L., & Gambrill, E. (2002). Evidence-based practice: Counterarguments to objections. *Research on Social Work Practice, 12*(3), 452–476.

Goodheart, C. D. (2006). Evidence, endeavor, and expertise in psychology practice. In C. D. Goodheart, A. E. Kazdin, & R. J. Sternberg (Eds.), *Evidence-based Psychotherapy: Where Practice and Research Meet* (pp. 37–61). Washington, DC: American Psychological Association. https://doi.org/10.1037/11423-002

Guyatt, G. H., Sackett, D. L., Sinclair, J. C., Hayward, R., Cook, D. J., Cook, R. J., … Wilson, M. (1995). Users' guides to the medical literature. *JAMA, 274*(22), 1800. https://doi.org/10.1001/jama.1995.03530220066035

Jones, J. L., & Mehr, S. L. (2007). Foundations and assumptions of the scientist-practitioner model. *American Behavioral Scientist, 50*(6), 766–771. https://doi.org/10.1177/0002764206296454

Lilienfeld, S. O., Ritschel, L. A., Lynn, S. J., Cautin, R. L., & Latzman, R. D. (2013). Why many clinical psychologists are resistant to evidence-based practice: Root causes and constructive remedies. *Clinical Psychology Review, 33*(7), 883–900. https://doi.org/10.1016/j.cpr.2012.09.008

Long, C. G., & Hollin, C. R. (1997). The scientist practitioner model in clinical psychology: A critique. *Clinical Psychology and Psychotherapy, 4*, 7583. https://doi.org/10.1002/cpp.5640020305

Norcross, J. C., & Karpiak, C. P. (2012). Clinical psychologists in the 2010s: 50 years of the APA Division of Clinical Psychology. *Clinical Psychology Science and Practice, 19*(1), 1–12. https://doi.org/10.1111/j.1468-2850.2012.01269.x

Parry, G., Cape, J., & Pilling, S. (2003). Clinical practice guidelines in clinical psychology and psychotherapy. *Clinical Psychology and Psychotherapy, 10*(6), 337–351. https://doi.org/10.1002/cpp.381

Petty, N. J. (2015). Becoming an expert: A masterclass in developing clinical expertise. *International Journal of Osteopathic Medicine, 18*(3), 207–218. https://doi.org/10.1016/j.ijosm.2015.01.001

Sackett, D. L. (1997). Evidence-based medicine. *Seminars in Perinatology, 21*(1), 3–5. https://doi.org/10.1016/S0146-0005(97)80013-4

Sackett, D. L., Rosenberg, W. M., Gray, J. A., Haynes, R. B., & Richardson, W. S. (1996). Evidence based medicine: What it is and what it isn't. *BMJ (Clinical Research ed.), 312*(7023), 71–72. https://doi.org/10.1136/BMJ.312.7023.71

Seligman, M. E. P. (1995). The effectiveness of psychotherapy: The Consumer Reports study. *American Psychologist, 50*(12), 965–974. https://doi.org/10.1037/0003-066X.50.12.965

Spring, B. (2007). Evidence-based practice in clinical psychology: What it is, why it matters; what you need to know. *Journal of Clinical Psychology, 63*(7), 611–631. https://doi.org/10.1002/jclp.20373

Stirman, S. W., Gutner, C. A., Crits-Christoph, P., Edmunds, J., Evans, A. C., & Beidas, R. S. (2015). Relationships between clinician-level attributes and fidelity-consistent and fidelity-inconsistent modifications to an evidence-based psychotherapy. *Implementation Science*, 10, Art. 115, 13 August. https://doi.org/10.1186/s13012-015-0308-z

Task Force on Promotion and Dissemination of Psychological Procedures. (1995). Training in and dissemination of empirically validated psychological treatments: Report and recommendations. *The Clinical Psychologist, 48*(1), 3–23.

Tolin, D. F., McKay, D., Forman, E. M., Klonsky, E. D., & Thombs, B. D. (2015). Empirically supported treatment: Recommendations for a new model. *Clinical Psychology Science and Practice, 22*(4), 317–338. https://doi.org/10.1111/cpsp.12122

Woodbridge, B., & Fulford, K. (2004). *Whose Values? A Workbook for Values-based Practice in Mental Health Care.* Retrieved from www.scmh.org.uk

Woolf, S. H., Grol, R., Hutchinson, A., Eccles, M., & Grimshaw, J. (1999). Clinical guidelines: Potential benefits, limitations, and harms of clinical guidelines. *BMJ* (Clinical Research ed.), *318*(7182), 527–530. https://doi.org/10.1136/BMJ.318.7182.527

2

Multidisciplinary Teams

On reading this chapter you will:

- Understand the rationale for multidisciplinary team working
- Understand the function of multidisciplinary teams
- Understand what makes an effective team
- Appreciate the importance of communication
- Understand the potential for conflict in multidisciplinary teams as well as issues related to relationship boundaries and power imbalances
- Appreciate how conflict can change organisational processes and culture
- Be aware of your role in a multidisciplinary team

Introduction

Multidisciplinary teams make up the core of organisations such as the National Health Service (NHS) and local authorities (LAs). Community support became the mainstay of health and social care services following the National Health Service and Community Care Act (1990), which required local authorities to help vulnerable adults (and their carers) remain in the community. In doing so, there was an increased need for the NHS to provide services in the community. The solution, to serve the needs of the population, the organisation and the law, was to bring groups of professionals together with the sole purpose of providing a service to a particular group of the population in a cohesive and cost-efficient manner. With improved collaboration across professional disciplines, care outcomes were shown to improve. There is evidence that multidisciplinary teams are effective in facilitating collaboration (Jones, 2006), thus improving care outcomes. Such teams can be spread across multiple locations, and there is no particular rule on what a multidisciplinary team should look like.

On first hearing the term 'multidisciplinary team', the casual observer may assume that it relates to a group of professionals working together. Although this is essentially accurate, there is far more to consider when looking at the form, function and success of a multidisciplinary team. To add to the complexity, which will be discussed within this chapter, when exploring the literature, we come across two terms – 'multidisciplinary' and 'interdisciplinary' – which can be confusing, particularly as they are often used interchangeably. For the purposes of this chapter, we will use the term 'multidisciplinary', where the care given to service users is drawn from knowledge across different disciplines, each providing input related to their area of expertise. Interdisciplinary work involves the sharing of specialist knowledge and authority with the intention of meeting the needs of the service user (Carrier & Kendall, 1995).

Multidisciplinary teams within healthcare services

- There is a team manager or practice lead whose role is to facilitate the relationship between the organisation and the team, the relationships among team members, and the relationship between the organisation, team and service user.
- Regular team meetings are held to ensure that the team meets its objectives in providing a service to service users (e.g. referrals and the sharing of organisational and team information and concerns).
- Team members with the appropriate skillset contribute to the process of assessment and intervention, ensuring a coherent service based on regular information sharing.
- Where packages of care are complex, a 'care coordinator' is identified among team members to ensure that service provision is managed effectively.

Multidisciplinary Team Objectives

Choi and Pak (2006) state that the objectives of multidisciplinary working encompass the following: (1) to find a resolution for complex problems, (2) to allow for different perspectives, (3) to develop a comprehensive approach to research and practice, and (4) to agree on clinical definitions and clinical guidelines across disciplines. How do multidisciplinary teams achieve these objectives? Let us first consider the function of teams.

According to Franklin, Bernhardt, Lopez, Long-Middleton and Davis (2015), there is an assumption that a team approach can achieve what an individual cannot. Team work can lead to better cost-efficiency through less duplication of tasks. Franklin and colleagues suggest the following as key elements of team work:

- Shared responsibility for goals and outcomes.
- Tasks that can be shared among all team members.
- A commitment to a shared approach.
- Collective management.

These key factors are therefore the foundation of effective teams. Of course, the success of such elements is somewhat dependent on the team itself, its structure, membership, division of roles, common values, and so forth. At their core, teams need to embody trust, respect and collaboration.

There is a dynamic essence within all teams and this is outlined by Tuckman's (1965) developmental model of group formation. The model is made up of a sequential path through four areas of change: (1) forming, (2) storming, (3) norming, and (4) performing. According to Tuckman, *forming* involves pushing boundaries within relationships and tasks, and *storming* involves conflict around interpersonal issues. In *norming*, such resistance is overcome, with group members settling into their respective roles. Finally, *performing*, as the name suggests, is where the group energy is cohesive, tasks get done and the group functions as it should. What is central to this model is the focus on relationships. It is not a linear model in practice. Teams and groups do not go through such an orderly sequence and ultimately perform; teams change, as do people, and therefore Tuckman's model can be seen as a dynamic cycle which encompasses change within teams.

Effective Multidisciplinary Teams

Mickan and Rodger (2000) outline 18 characteristics of successful and effective teams across three contexts: (1) organisational structure, (2) individual contribution, and (3) team processes. Mickan and Rodger suggest that organisational structure interventions lead to better outcomes than process interventions when dealing with teams that are not functioning well. The subsequent positive impact on team processes leads to improved individual contributions. However, in the same way that the development of a team is not linear, there is also a dynamic quality in the ever-changing relationship between organisational structure and team process.

Organisational characteristics of multidisciplinary teams

According to Mickan and Rodger (2000), the organisational characteristics of multi-disciplinary teams are:

- Purpose – there is a mission statement, and shared values and goals.
- Culture – comprising recognition and integration within the organisation, behavioural norms and shared success.
- Task – the team needs to make a tangible contribution to the organisation which fits within the team's purpose.
- Roles – there are distinct roles which are flexible enough to accommodate individual differences.
- Suitable leadership – the development of a strategic focus with the team goals and values at the core of any activity or change.
- Appropriate team members – comprising a heterogeneity of skills, interests and backgrounds across different professions.
- Resources – comprising education, administrative and technical support, and financial resources.

Models of effectiveness

So that we can place team working in context, one of the most useful tools is to look at models of team effectiveness, or what makes a *good* team. These models are a diagrammatic representation of key characteristics similar to those outlined by Mickan and Rodger (2000). Such models have existed since Rubin, Plovnick and Fry (1977) proposed the Goals, Roles, Processes and Interpersonal Relationships (GRPI) model. The GRPI model is in the form of a triangle, with each characteristic of an effective team placed in order of importance. At the heart of the pyramid is 'interpersonal relationships', where good communication, trust and flexibility are key and uphold the procedures, roles and goals of the team, thus characterising an effective team. Due in part to its simplicity, the GRPI model is considered useful when first setting up a team or in dealing with problematic issues that may arise (more of this later). As in Tuckman's (1965) model, the relationships among team members are the cornerstone of good multidisciplinary teams. We therefore need to consider factors that may hinder such relationships and ways to manage or overcome such issues.

Other models exist, such as those suggested by Katzenbach and Smith (1993), LaFasto and Larson (2001), Hackman (2002) and Lencioni (2005). These offer different levels of complexity yet are all touching on similar themes. The reader is encouraged to look at these different models and to form their own view. Based on the characteristics that most often appear in models of effectiveness, the remainder of this chapter will focus on communication, conflict and conflict resolution, organisational culture, professional boundaries and power.

Communication

There are many factors that can be described as promoting effective team working, specifically, what makes a *good* team. According to Ruhstaller, Roe, Thürlimann and Nicoll (2006), communication in multidisciplinary teams is one such factor and can directly impact the quality of care given to service users. Multidisciplinary team working is based on communication and collaboration, and therefore the methods used to facilitate this are paramount.

Multidisciplinary team meetings

Most multidisciplinary teams will have a weekly meeting, which can range from 30 minutes to a whole morning. The number of attendees is generally fewer than 20 team members, although it depends on the size of the team. The purpose of such meetings can include distributing referrals and discussing individual cases, communicating organisational news, discussing practical issues (where have all the teaspoons gone?), and they provide an opportunity for everyone to spend time with one another (which can foster good working relationships and a sense of community). However, while a weekly meeting may seem useful, whether or not such meetings do actually promote good communication and tangible service outcomes can be a matter of debate.

It is important that the discussions that take place in these meetings are documented so that team members can see management plans and important information. Not only is this important for the team and organisation, but it is absolutely essential for planning and ensuring service user care. However, problems occur due to a lack of administrative resources for minuting such meetings, and individual notes in service user files following the meetings may not fully and accurately reflect the outcome of the team discussion. Any ambiguity can lead to disastrous outcomes for the service user, where confusion as to who should contact whom and who should be involved with the next step of care can lead to delays and, in the worst cases, be entirely overlooked. Another important function of shared multidisciplinary meeting notes is to allow those who may miss the meeting to catch up. For some staff members, non-attendance is inevitable, perhaps because they work part time, for example, or are a trainee on placement for a few days each week. Other problems that can arise include the folllowing:

- Unnecessary chat, which is more social in nature but which can mask the central message of the discussion.

- Whoever takes the notes must have a knowledge of professional terminology and style, so that there is no confusion in translating such information to note form.
- There must be agreement on what the notes should focus on. For example, if it is 'next steps', then this is what should be noted.

Your role in a multidisciplinary team meeting

When you are unfamiliar with multidisciplinary team meetings within an organisation, whether this is because you have only just finished training or you are in a new job, there are a few hints and tips that might make this a little easier. It is perfectly natural to feel nervous, particularly if you are unsure of expectations. You can prepare yourself in the following ways:

- Know the details of who is attending and how long the meeting will be.
- If you can talk to one of your colleagues about the nature of these meetings and possible historical issues, this can help (you can be honest about your fears!).
- Make sure you understand your role and your responsibilities.
- You can prepare and take some notes into the meeting, which can act as a prompt (even if you don't use them, preparing them in advance can help you with your confidence and to clarify your thoughts).
- You may want to observe rather than contribute in the first meeting so that you can become familiar in the process, or you can contribute by asking questions if there is something you are unsure about (sometimes these questions can wait until after the meeting).
- Be respectful and do not dominate the discussion.
- If you do not have the answer to a question asked of you, it is better to say that you do not know (this is OK, we cannot know everything).

Conflict and Conflict Resolution

It is natural for there to be conflict at one time or another in any group. It can be described as emerging from differences in values, ideas and beliefs among team members. Conflict can certainly result in negative outcomes for team cohesion or for service outcomes, particularly service user care. However, conflict can also result in positive outcomes, where approaching an issue in a measured and controlled manner, and acknowledging the need for change where this is necessary, can lead to better organisational or service user outcomes. To work within a multidisciplinary team, you need to understand conflict resolution as well as have good self-awareness and good communication skills. When beginning a new role in an organisation, an understanding of conflict resolution policies can be useful.

According to the British Psychological Society's *Practice Guidelines* (2017), for psychologists working in multidisciplinary teams, resolution should involve clear communication, evidence, and a collaborative partnership between those involved in resolving issues through respectful argument. Although this advice is written specifically for the practitioner psychologist, it remains the same for any professional faced with a similar situation. It is advised that the matter is first discussed in confidence between those involved in the conflict. It is also suggested that this is done in a calm and helpful manner, with the appropriate and relevant information. Advice can also be sought from more experienced colleagues; or in situations where there is serious continued disagreement, then both parties can approach the appropriate supervisor or line manager to arbitrate. Written records should be kept at all stages. This can avoid any confusion and can limit the emotionality that inevitably arises in such situations. In cases of reported *bad practice*, supervisors or line managers have a duty from a professional standards and organisational perspective and should approach the practitioner in question and inform them of the concerns before notifying the relevant professional body or organisation contact.

Conflict can sometimes occur as a result of a lack of awareness or understanding of the different professional roles within the multidisciplinary team. It is recommended that when beginning to work in a multidisciplinary setting, you make yourself aware of all duties and responsibilities, and indeed the ethos, of each profession you work with. The most effective way of doing this, of course, is to talk to your colleagues. There may be official descriptions of professional roles, but there will be personal nuances relevant to each of your colleagues.

According to Firth-Cozens (2001), conflict can occur where there are disagreements on what constitutes a good outcome. Such issues can be overcome by sharing information on the range of potential outcomes, e.g. greater service user functionality versus quality of life versus carer needs, and what constitutes success. Also noted by Firth-Cozens (2001) is professional allegiance, to both the team and to one's profession. This is particularly salient where there is management involvement in the areas of complaint. To overcome any professional barriers, it is suggested that the focus should be placed firmly on the service users and their values – specifically, what constitutes a good outcome for them.

Other aspects of team working that can cause conflict are interpersonal difficulties between team members. The mix of professional roles and personal relationships among team members can sometimes cause difficulty as miscommunication and perceived slights lead to offence. For example, a person who is newly appointed to a managerial role and becomes detached from other team members may be perceived as lacking warmth and choosing to no longer mix with colleagues who they were once close with; in fact it is more likely that the newly appointed manager, in trying to manage a new role and responsibilities, is just too busy. Such conflict can be difficult to manage but, as professionals, we need to be able to identify and challenge problematic relationships between professional colleagues. Good social relationships among colleagues lead to an effective team. Team members can be key in sharing information, providing practical support, helping with problems and finding solutions. Most importantly, positive social relationships in the workplace can guard against stress and burnout (Mickan & Rodger, 2000).

Conflict can also occur between the individual practitioner and the team's goals and values (or lack thereof). This can result from a lack of understanding of what the team's goals are or because there is disagreement between personal values and those of the team. In cases where there is a lack of understanding, this can be because there is no clear statement of values and goals (and thus poor cohesion) or because communication of what those values and goals are is poor. It is always beneficial to foster cohesion among team members, and smaller team sizes and physical proximity are to be encouraged (Mickan & Rodger, 2000). A team that is distributed across different sites or organisations, or some of whose members have their own office while others have to share office space, can cause rifts and power imbalances, and therefore have a direct impact on team cohesion. It is always advised that multidisciplinary teams receive training on teamwork and team building, and especially in what this constitutes within a healthcare setting. Team 'away days' can also foster cohesion, particularly if the 'away day' is centred on activities that have no bearing on the day-to-day tasks of the job (e.g. undertaking survival challenges).

One of the greatest difficulties that multidisciplinary teams face is the resource of time, upon which the central tenants of collaboration, trust and respect are formed. So that individual team members can appreciate the importance of listening to each other, value should be placed on the information that is shared, and practitioners should have the confidence to engage in clear, two-way communication within and outside the team. Time should be allocated for this to occur. As a professional in any organisation, and in accordance with professional standards and personal values, we should have the confidence to challenge organisations where there is a lack of importance (and therefore time) placed on communication. At a time when health and social care services are being pushed to perform and produce tangible outcomes, it is difficult to push against the tide, but every effort should be made to do so. Although teams can have a cohesive structure, good communication, trust and respect, it is ultimately the organisational structure that can foster development or protect against dysfunction.

Organisational Culture

Organisational culture can impact greatly on service implementation and outcomes. Simply put, organisational culture is the way things are done in an organisation. A survey conducted by Glisson et al. (2008) explored organisational culture across three dimensions: (1) organisational expectation and priority, (2) the wellbeing of staff, and (3) staff commitment. Culture is how we understand and interpret the organisation (Parmelli et al., 2011). It is essential that the organisation takes the lead in assessing and identifying areas of improvement in their multidisciplinary teams. It should be a *top-down* rather than a *bottom-up* process. There is nothing to stop a member of staff challenging organisational structures and alerting clinical and administrative management to any issues therein. Methods that can inform those in charge can consist of surveys, focus groups or suggestion boxes, to name but a few. Informal methods can be casual conversation, which may prompt further investigation into areas of concern. Ultimately, there needs to be clear leadership that is collaborative and team-driven. It is clear, though, that team members will only share such information when there is a culture of openness, trust and safety.

An organisation needs to have a set of policies and procedures which cover the key areas of organisational responsibility, including staff grievances. It is the responsibility of team members to become aware of these policies. Multidisciplinary team meetings can be a forum where these policies are discussed and reviewed. Organisations should conduct the necessary training, and hold regular sessions where employees are encouraged to discuss service user safety, employee safety, equality and diversity, and health and safety issues. Ideally, training on communication and team working, stress management, assertiveness and conflict management could be arranged. As a practitioner psychologist, adhering to the regulations of your professional body and maintaining a record of continuing professional development (CPD) will encourage you to notice any problems within the organisation. Multidisciplinary teams with a commitment to ongoing training foster a sense of trust and respect.

Effective multidisciplinary team working

For effective multidisciplinary team working, organisations should:

- Welcome diversity as a chance for creativity.
- Embrace conflict as an opportunity for change.
- Be clear on expectations and have policies and procedures in place.
- Support multidisciplinary teams with relationship building and opportunities for training and continuing professional development.
- Encourage a collaborative, two-way system of communication.
- Ensure a *top-down* approach in identifying any issues.
- Support staff and employee wellbeing.
- Have clear structures.

Professional Boundaries

Working in health and social care requires that the psychologist takes on a number of different roles. When working with other professions in a multidisciplinary team, the psychologist will have the professional status of the profession, in addition to a variety of other possible roles, as follows:

- Employee (organisational role)
- Colleague (team role)
- Friend (social relationship role)
- Therapist (organisational role)
- Professional body member (stakeholder role)
- Supervisor (organisational role).

It is therefore important that attention is given to the boundaries placed upon each role and that the potential blurring of these boundaries, which can occur in professional life, is acknowledged. Liberati, Gorli and Scaratti (2016) offer a useful overview of professional boundaries and the issues therein. The authors describe professional boundaries as 'socially constructed demarcations', which describe a profession's area of competence and what practitioners can and cannot do. It can be abused when one profession criticises the limitations of another, or even discounts the necessity of their area of competence in its entirety. The occurrence of such issues has been supported by the research literature (e.g. Martin, Currie, & Finn, 2009) and offers a stark reality for those working in multidisciplinary teams.

As has already been mentioned, a factor related to effective team working is trust. Each role demands that the psychologist develops a trusting relationship with other team members. However, that trust can be challenged. For example, what if a psychologist who has a friendship with a fellow professional becomes concerned about their practice? In what way would that be different from a situation where the person is a colleague rather than a friend?

Professional relationships and boundaries

According to the British Psychological Society's *Practice Guidelines* (BPS, 2017), the practitioner psychologist should do the following:

- Manage relationships in relation to context; i.e. in a professional setting, the relationship should remain professional even if colleagues have a close friendship outside of work.
- Recognise that potential conflicts of interest or ethical considerations could arise when there are multiple roles within the one relationship.
- Ensure that relevant stakeholders (e.g. employer) are made aware of relationships that cross boundaries so that any impact on professional roles is mitigated.

Power

There are also potential issues arising from imbalances in power. For example, consider a potential friendship between a clinical supervisor and a trainee Clinical Psychologist. In the role of supervisor, the psychologist has the power to pass or fail that trainee's placement. Would it be appropriate to decline supervising the trainee or would it suffice to have an open and frank discussion with the trainee and the clinical psychology programme beforehand? The general advice is to avoid having a professional relationship with someone when there has been or is a *close* personal relationship. How could you define *close*? It is inevitable that personal relationships will develop within work environments. However, it does not always bode well for the team when personal relationships do occur and are not dealt with correctly.

Not only do personal relationships have the ability to blur boundaries. Hierarchies within organisations, and indeed within multidisciplinary teams, are typically unavoidable since status and pay influence who gets the most respect (or who demands respect). Of course, levels of responsibility and competence do generally increase with status and pay, so such expectation is not without reason. However, hierarchies within multidisciplinary teams do create barriers and potential imbalances of power. One of the most problematic factors facing many teams – and where boundaries can become difficult – is workload. If one member of the team feels that they have greater demands placed on their time than others in the team, it can lead to anger and resentment. To manage such a situation requires the organisation to acknowledge that if the need for the skills of one particular profession within the team – occupational therapy, for example – outweighs the number of occupational therapists on the team, then this needs to be addressed. Equally, the practitioner who feels overwhelmed by their workload needs support and guidance from the wider team and from regular supervision. Care should be taken as the situation may have occurred as a result of personal, rather than organisational, factors. Such issues should be dealt with explicitly rather than behind closed doors, where further resentment may occur. With a focus on the overall team purpose, rather than individual contributions, the team can become a supportive environment.

The core principles of effective team working mean that team roles must incorporate the shared values and goals of the different professions that make up the multidisciplinary team. This includes perceived workload and other competing factors. How do we maintain professional integrity in such circumstances? The answer lies in working as a team, for the benefit of the team, communicating the core values of your profession as part of the team, maintaining an open and honest approach through ongoing clinical supervision and continuing professional development, and demonstrating leadership skills.

Summary

For the practitioner psychologist, then, how do we work in environments where there are both barriers and facilitators to effective team working? There are ways of working that can help you as a practitioner and the wider team in establishing appropriate boundaries, agreeing team identity and goals, establishing clear roles, ensuring appropriate communication, and working with conflict. The following steps can be useful for individuals who are joining an established team, who are in the process of setting up a new team, or who are influencing the practice of a current team.

- Allow yourself time to get to know the team, even if you have worked for the organisation for some time. We can sometimes fall into repeated patterns of functioning which we do not question.
- Talk to members of the team and establish with them what their perceived role is. Showing an interest can enable you to develop better relationships with members of the team that you rarely work with. Include all staff, especially those in administrative roles, as they are often the ones with the most knowledge of processes and procedures.
- Make yourself aware of procedures and policies, and take note of guidance that is out of date or procedures that should be present but are not.
- Take the opportunity to attend training on topics that could be useful, such as assertiveness, leadership and team effectiveness. If there is no training available, suggest that training is provided or, if possible, arrange training with the agreement of those in management roles.
- Suggest that team working is a regular item on the agenda in team meetings. This may not be given priority due to time pressures, but the working of the team can have a direct impact on service user care.
- As a scientist-practitioner, use your research skills to explore team functioning in more depth by conducting surveys, focus groups or research on the introduction of a novel approach to a particular aspect of team working. This may be limited due to time constraints, but a possible partnership with a trainee Clinical Psychologist or other team member may overcome this limitation.

As a practitioner psychologist, you hold many skills that can navigate the sometimes stormy waters of team environments. This chapter has covered many of the issues (and positives) of working within a multidisciplinary team. Not only do you need to consider the content of this chapter when beginning a new role in a multidisciplinary team, or when training; there should also be a continuing dialogue related to multidisciplinary team working from your personal and professional perspective, the personal and professional perspective of your colleagues, and the aims of the organisation. At the core is your wellbeing, and you are advised to read the chapters on supervision, reflective practice, leadership, and practitioner resilience to underpin your knowledge of multidisciplinary team working.

Key Points

- Multidisciplinary teams are the core means through which health and social care providers provide services.
- Multidisciplinary teams bring together a range of professional knowledge so that the service user receives the most comprehensive and appropriate care.
- Interventions aimed at changing organisational structure lead to better team functioning.
- The key characteristics necessary for effective team working are (1) purpose, (2) culture, (3) task, (4) roles, (5) leadership, (6) appropriate membership and (7) resources.
- Multidisciplinary team meetings are essential for sharing crucial information and determining the next steps in service user care.
- You have a key role in representing your profession and expertise in multidisciplinary team meetings.
- Conflict among team members is a natural occurrence and, if dealt with appropriately, can lead to positive outcomes.
- Organisational culture is key in supporting multidisciplinary teams and in providing the necessary resources (e.g. policies, guidelines, training).
- Professional boundaries and power issues can derail the functioning of teams. Action should be explicit, and it is advised that such issues are identified (as far as is possible) before such issues occur.

Practice Case Studies

Case Study 1

You recently started working with a Child and Adolescent Mental Health team as a Clinical Psychologist. This is your first job since qualifying. You enjoy your work and thrive on the challenges it provides. You feel you have a good working relationship with your colleagues, who are a mix of social workers, mental health nurses and Clinical Psychologists.

You and a senior Clinical Psychologist are working on an initiative with local schools where you offer training for teachers on what to do when a student discloses self-harm. The training package has been put together by the senior Clinical Psychologist and is delivered by both of you. A number of issues have arisen where you feel that the content of the training package could be improved, based on your own experience and research, and the evaluation feedback provided by teachers who have attended the training. You feel strongly that the training should be developed in collaboration with the schools.

However, the senior Clinical Psychologist does not feel that any changes need to be made, despite your tentative suggestions. You are further conflicted as the senior Clinical Psychologist is a good friend as well as a colleague, and you often spend time together out of work.

Balancing this conflict is proving difficult and you find yourself becoming stressed and avoiding your friend and colleague. This morning you have received a phone call from the head teacher of one of the schools where the training has been delivered who has voiced their concerns about the content as it contradicts school policy.

Suggested questions

1. There are a number of shared roles between you and the senior Clinical Psychologist. In what way could this situation have been managed prior to you beginning this piece of work?
2. What would be your next step in this situation? How would you ensure the best outcome for the school?

Case Study 2

You have been working as a Health Psychologist at a local general hospital for two years. You are part of a team of social workers and the only Health Psychologist on the team. You have developed good working relationships with consultants and ward staff, who regularly refer patients to you.

Your role in the team is to help patients with psychological issues arising from chronic health conditions, such as non-adherence to medication, coping with their diagnosis, etc. The social workers you work with are friendly and you meet weekly to discuss referrals and upcoming discharges for patients referred to your team. Although your work is somewhat different from that of the other team members (social workers focus on discharge and ongoing care in the community), you often discuss patients and organisational issues.

You have noticed over previous months that many of the referrals made to the team have to wait longer than is appropriate and you are concerned that this has a negative impact on patient care. Team members appear overworked and unmotivated, and the team manager (who is a social worker) does not seem to address these issues. Your clinical supervisor, who is a more experienced Health Psychologist at another hospital, meets you monthly.

Suggested questions

1. What are the primary problems within this particular multidisciplinary team? Who should take responsibility and why?
2. What could be done to promote a positive change? How would you do this?

References

British Psychological Society. (2017). *Practice Guidelines*. Leicester, UK: BPS. Retrieved from www.bps.org.uk/sites/www.bps.org.uk/files/Policy/Policy%20-%20Files/BPS%20Practice%20Guidelines%20%28Third%20Edition%29.pdf

Carrier, J., & Kendall, I. (1995). Professionalism and interprofessionalism in health and community care: Some theoretical issues. In *Interprofessional Issues in Community and Primary Health Care* (pp. 9–36). London: Macmillan. https://doi.org/10.1007/978-1-349-13236-2_2

Choi, B. C. K., & Pak, A. W. P. (2006). Multidisciplinarity, interdisciplinarity and transdisciplinarity in health research, services, education and policy: 1. Definitions, objectives, and evidence of effectiveness. *Clinical and Investigative Medicine/Médecine Clinique et Expérimentale*, *29*(6), 351–364. Retrieved from www.ncbi.nlm.nih.gov/pubmed/17330451

Department of Health. (1990). *National Health Service and Community Care Act (1990)*. London: HMSO. Available at https://www.legislation.gov.uk/ukpga/1990/19/contents (accessed: 2 February 2021).

Firth-Cozens, J. (2001). Multidisciplinary teamwork: The good, bad, and everything in between. *Quality in Health Care*, *10*(2), 65–66. https://doi.org/10.1136/qhc.10.2.65

Franklin, C. M., Bernhardt, J. M., Lopez, R. P., Long-Middleton, E. R., & Davis, S. (2015). Interprofessional teamwork and collaboration between community health workers and healthcare teams: An integrative review. *Health Services Research and Managerial Epidemiology*, *2*, doi:10.1177/2333392815573312.

Glisson, C., Landsverk, J., Schoenwald, S., Kelleher, K., Hoagwood, K. E., Mayberg, S., . . . Research Network on Youth Mental Health. (2008). Assessing the Organizational Social Context (OSC) of mental health services: Implications for research and practice. *Administration and Policy in Mental Health and Mental Health Services Research*, *35*(1–2), 98–113. doi:10.1007/s10488-007-0148-5.

Hackman, J. R., (2002). *Leading Teams: Setting the Stage for Great Performances*. Boston, MA: Harvard Business Press.

Jones, A. (2006). Multidisciplinary team working: Collaboration and conflict. *International Journal of Mental Health Nursing*, March. https://doi.org/10.1111/j.1447-0349.2006.00400.x

Katzenbach, J. R., & Smith, D. K. (1993). The rules for managing cross-functional reengineering teams. *Planning Review*, *21*(2), 12–13.

LaFasto, F., & Larson, C. (2001). *When Teams Work Best: 6,000 Team Members and Leaders Tell What It Takes to Succeed*. London: Sage.

Lencioni, P. (2005). *Overcoming the Five Dysfunctions of a Team*. San Fransisco, CA: Jossey-Bass.

Liberati, E. G., Gorli, M., & Scaratti, G. (2016). Invisible walls within multidisciplinary teams: Disciplinary boundaries and their effects on integrated care. *Social Science & Medicine*, *150*, 31–39. https://doi.org/10.1016/j.socscimed.2015.12.002

Martin, G. P., Currie, G., & Finn, R. (2009). Reconfiguring or reproducing intra-professional boundaries? Specialist expertise, generalist knowledge and the 'modernization' of the medical workforce. *Social Science & Medicine*, *68*(7), 1191–1198.

Mickan, S., & Rodger, S. (2000). Characteristics of effective teams: A literature review. *Australian Health Review*, *23*(3), 201. https://doi.org/10.1071/AH000201

Parmelli, E., Flodgren, G., Beyer, F., Baillie, N., Schaafsma, M. E., & Eccles, M. P. (2011). The effectiveness of strategies to change organisational culture to improve healthcare performance: A systematic review. *Implementation Science, 6*(1), 33. https://doi.org/10.1186/1748-5908-6-33

Rubin, I. M., Plovnick, M. S., & Fry, R. E. (1977). *Task-oriented Team Development.* New York: McGraw-Hill.

Ruhstaller, T., Roe, H., Thürlimann, B., & Nicoll, J. J. (2006). The multidisciplinary meeting: An indispensable aid to communication between different specialities. *European Journal of Cancer, 42*(15), 2459–2462. https://doi.org/10.1016/J.EJCA.2006.03.034

Tuckman, B. W. (1965). Developmental sequence in small groups. *Psychological Bulletin, 63.* doi:10.1037/H0022100. Retrieved from https://web.mit.edu/curhan/www/docs/Articles/15341_Readings/Group_Dynamics/Tuckman_1965_Developmental_sequence_in_small_groups.pdf

3

Supervision

On reading this chapter you will:

- Understand the purpose of clinical supervision
- Understand the format and process of clinical supervision
- Understand your role as a supervisee
- Understand your role as a supervisor
- Appreciate the complexity of the supervisory relationship
- Appreciate the requirement for competence in clinical supervision
- Understand the challenges and key issues of engaging fully in clinical supervision

Introduction

Clinical supervision is a critical aspect of working as a practitioner psychologist. Supervision is a formal requirement where the practitioner meets with a trained supervisor (within the same profession) who, according to Milne (2007), offers support, aids career development, and manages and evaluates the progression of the supervisee. There are many professional guidelines and models which aim to guide the process of supervision and these can be helpful, but it is the supervisory relationship that determines whether the aims of supervision are achieved. The aim of this chapter is to outline what skills are required of supervisors (and supervisees), the importance of the supervisory relationship, the *how* and *how not* to engage in supervision, and to highlight the challenges of the supervisory role.

When using the term 'supervision', care should be taken to distinguish between different types of organisational supervision. In this chapter, we use 'supervision' to refer to clinical supervision. Other types of supervision that can be commonly confused with clinical supervision are line management supervision and professional supervision. It is usual for the practitioner psychologist to have separate supervisors that undertake these roles. For example, the team manager will undertake line management duties and will typically be a non-psychologist. Professional supervision focuses on personal development plans, organisational appraisal, continuing professional development (CPD) within the profession, professional practice standards and ethics and codes of conduct (British Psychological Society, 2014). In some organisations, a single supervisor will undertake both professional and clinical supervisory roles.

There is not just one approach to conducting supervision. In addition to the traditional one-to-one format, there are more organisationally friendly approaches, such as group supervision (whether peer-led or led by a lead supervisor). Remote supervision can also be conducted using online means (e.g. Skype, telephone or email). Live supervision is another alternative, where the supervisor sits-in in a session between the supervisee and service user. Although one-to-one supervision should remain the primary goal, in the organisational context, some of these methods can overcome resource limitations, where supervisory time is limited. For example, group supervision saves the time that would be involved in providing each member of that group with one-to-one supervision. Yet there are also drawbacks with such alternative methods, particularly when we consider the importance of the supervisory relationship, which is much easier to develop on a one-to-one basis.

When we explore the function of supervision, there are three (at a minimum) areas to consider:

- **Supervision and the service user:** Ultimately, the primary aim of supervision is to protect the service user. The supervisor should ensure that the work of the supervisee meets professional standards. The process of supervision therefore has a key organisational function.
- **Supervision and the practitioner:** The practitioner can use the supervision space and the support of the supervisor to reflect upon professional activities. As discussed in Chapter 7 on reflective practice, this process aims to increase self-awareness. With effective supervision, the supervisor can guide the supervisee in developing their reflective practice. Not only is reflective practice key in ensuring that the practitioner engages in correct practice, it serves as a self-care tool in that the risk of burnout is openly discussed and appropriate measures can be put in place to protect the wellbeing of the supervisee.
- **Supervision and the supervisor:** It is an expectation in the healthcare sector that practitioner psychologists engage in supervisory duties. This can be a daunting task for early career practitioners, but is also a major factor in professional development. Indeed, the practice of supervising a less experienced peer can lead to professional development gains for the supervisor and the opportunity to re-energise their own practice.

Ethical Principles of Supervision

With a focus on the safety of the service user and supervisee (supervisors are also supervisees), we enter the realm of ethical practice and the elements that are necessary for the process and function of supervision. Ethical factors are relevant for the service user, the supervisor and the supervisee.

- **Service user:** What is often missed is the acknowledgement of the need to gain, and indeed the practice of gaining, informed consent from the service user for the practitioner psychologist to discuss their particular case in supervision. This would involve telling the service user that the practitioner might discuss details of their case with their supervisor. It is advised that this discussion and its outcome are written in the case notes. It is also necessary to inform the service user that the practitioner is a trainee (if this is the case). Where supervisory methods include the recording (video/audio) and observation of service user sessions, explicit consent should be elicited from the service user (American Psychological Association, 2010).
- **Supervisor:** What is not often mentioned is that, typically, even early career practitioners (as early as 12 months following qualification) are expected to undertake the role of supervisor. It begs the question as to whether early career supervisors are competent enough to identify areas of concern or to guide the supervisee. Of course, the supervisor is also engaging in their own supervision with another colleague, which can mitigate these issues to some extent. Despite the professional requirements, though, to truly offer quality supervision is challenging, given stretched resources and limits on the number of experienced practitioners (such challenges will be discussed later in the chapter). It is also important that the supervisor has knowledge of the supervisee's caseload (particularly with trainees) so that the development of effective treatment plans can be closely monitored. For trainees, the supervisor holds the primary responsibility (signified in part by the requirement that the supervisor countersigns reports). The supervisor may also need to take over cases where an emergency arises or areas of risk develop that are beyond the competency of the trainee (or even early career practitioner). It is therefore important from an ethical standpoint that the supervisor does not take on more supervisees than they can comfortably (and safely) manage.
- **Supervisee:** As a supervisee, although difficult to monitor, it is ethical to bring all aspects of professional practice into supervision. This can be challenging (see the discussion of supervisory challenges), but can truly aid professional development. One of the main areas in which the supervisee can maintain the structure and function of the supervisory sessions is through making clear and concise notes of these meetings. Traditionally, even though it is the supervisor who might suggest this, convention dictates that it is the supervisee who takes notes during supervision sessions. It is also worthwhile for these notes to be signed by both the supervisor and supervisee at the end of the session as a true record of the main discussion points. Where discussion of a service user occurs, it is also suggested that the supervisee notes the discussion in the service user's file. This can avoid any potential issues at a later date.

Competence within the Supervision Relationship

From an ethical perspective, monitoring competence is an essential aspect of supervision. It is inherent in all guidelines and ethical codes across the mental health professions and in different countries (e.g. British Psychological Society, 2009). It is therefore an ethical requirement of supervisors (and sometimes a legal responsibility) to ensure that the supervisee is capable of the service that they deliver (Bernard & Goodyear, 2014). Competency-based supervision (where supervision serves the purpose of increasing practice-based skills) is therefore recommended. For example, an early career practitioner may not be able to manage a case effectively where there are elements of severe risk and supervision is minimal, whereas if the supervisee shadows the supervisor in working with such a case, a valuable learning opportunity presents itself and the case can serve as a learning experience (Thomas, 2010).

According to the Codes of Ethics and Conduct for practitioner psychologists (British Psychology Society, 2009), a further element that is within the obligation of supervisors is to monitor ethical practice. Despite there being a requirement on the supervisee to have knowledge of and engage in ethical practice, it is the supervisor who monitors whether the practitioner they supervise is aware of the ethical principles of the profession, e.g. we only know what we know; what is unknown never presents as a problem. Although those who are newly qualified in the profession have the benefit of recent training in ethical codes of practice, it is also true that they may not be aware of how to enact those requirements in practice. This is where good supervision is key.

It is also important that the supervisor is competent in providing clinical supervision as well as in the professional activities engaged in by the supervisee. For example, the supervisee may wish to be trained in, or may already be trained in, a skill where the supervisor has no experience, e.g. a particular therapeutic modality. The supervisee should not be discouraged from approaching the supervisor to request support in this situation; another clinical supervisor could be brought in to supervise this element of the supervisee's work. According to Thomas (2010), areas that may be relevant here include administering psychological tests or working with service users from a particular cultural background. What should not happen is that the supervisor places the responsibility for knowledge in that domain to the supervisee and *assumes* that the supervisee is the expert in that area.

Supervisory Contract

The supervisory contract aims to consolidate the requirements of supervision and is agreed collaboratively between the supervisor and supervisee (Luepker, 2012). It is an essential document, which can serve as a framework for both supervisor and supervisee on their roles and responsibilities. The British

Psychology Society (2014) provides a template of a supervisory contract, which includes the factors that should be considered. It should be noted, however, that each organisation will have unique requirements so any template should be amended as appropriate.

Supervisory contract

A supervisory contract should consider the following elements:

- The time, date, length and location of each supervision session (this should meet the professional guidelines for each profession and length of career).
- A statement of who will provide the supervision.
- A statement of who will arrange the location and who will book the space (typically the supervisor will arrange this).
- What happens if a session is cancelled?
- Who writes the notes, where will these be kept and by whom, how many copies will be made, who signs the document, etc.
- A statement of the supervisee's responsibilities. That is, what they should bring to supervision, e.g. concerns, training requirements, a readiness to engage, etc.
- A statement of the supervisor's responsibilities. That is, what they should bring to supervision, e.g. concerns, supervisory session structure, support, enthusiasm, and how they propose to monitor the supervisee's practice, such as using recordings of service user sessions, in-person observation of service user sessions, service user feedback.
- The need to be aware of professional requirements such as continuing professional development objectives, professional registration requirements (e.g. Health Care Professions Council) and organisational requirements (e.g. mandatory training, a review of the workload, the potential for risk and burnout).
- Methods of feedback and appraisal. This can be a challenging aspect of supervision and can have a positive or negative influence on the supervisory relationship. When preparing the supervisory contract, it is always useful for both parties to discuss what feedback will look like, what the appraisal requirements are, etc. Reflective practice and self-awareness are key here as we are all subject to individual differences in how we receive feedback, e.g. sometimes it can be difficult to receive and to *recognise* positive feedback.

Source: British Psychological Society (2014).

It is very worthwhile to ensure that such a contract is put together at the outset of supervision. It is also essential that the contract is monitored from time to time and that amendments are made as appropriate. The likelihood of such a contract existing is more likely for early career practitioners, but it cannot be underestimated that there are benefits in creating such a contract for more experienced practitioners – particularly as the longer we practise, the more we are likely to rely on tried-and-tested techniques and will fail to keep up with changing practices, policies or legal requirements.

The Effective Supervisor

Given the importance of supervision in how practitioners reflect, develop and engage in safe practice, it is essential that the supervisor is competent. So, what would an effective supervisor look like? The supervisor must show commitment to their role and in the development of the supervisee's professional competence. As we know, developing a strong therapeutic relationship is a key aspect of successful outcomes for service users (Howgego, Yellowlees, Owen, Meldrum, & Dark, 2003). It is therefore logical to presume that the relationship between supervisor and supervisee is crucial for success (Ladany, Ellis, & Friedlander, 1999; Wulf & Nelson, 2000).

The effective supervisor

Barnett, Erickson Cornish, Goodyear and Lichtenberg (2007) suggest that the following factors (adapted from Lowry, 2001) are necessary for effective supervision (and therefore on how to be an effective supervisor):

- That the supervisor has clinical skills and knowledge.
- That the supervisor is accepting.
- That the supervisor demonstrates the desire to engage in the supervisory process.
- That the supervisor is empathic.
- That the supervisor is flexible (this incorporates the personal and theoretical).
- That the supervisor is available.
- That the supervisor is knowledgeable and experienced (in theory, practice and supervision).

Ladany, Mori and Mehr (2013) explored the nature of effective and ineffective supervision and found that the supervisor should also be attentive and task-oriented and use self-disclosure appropriately. Self-disclosure can be useful to normalise the supervisee's clinical experience and professional identity (Clevinger, Albert, & Raiche, 2019), and can in some instances strengthen the supervisory relationship (Ladany & Lehrman-Waterman, 1999). In relation to feedback, this should be consistent with the set supervisory goals and provide both formative feedback (ongoing feedback while engaging in a task) and summative feedback (overall feedback at the end of a task).

The supervisor needs to acknowledge that the supervisee will have different needs at different stages of their career, where the supervisory needs of a practitioner in training will differ from the needs of a more experienced practitioner. There is also the question of a supervisor bringing their own supervisory experiences to supervision with their supervisor (you may have to read that sentence more than once). Is it therefore logical to have a continuum of supervisory experience – i.e. that the gap in knowledge between the supervisor and supervisee is not so large as to stretch the supervisory relationship beyond its limits? Unfortunately, such consideration may be impossible in an overstretched organisation. Nevertheless, open and honest communication between the supervisor and supervisee should acknowledge the impact of such issues on the relationship.

Therapeutic Modalities in Supervision

Supervision can be led by therapeutic approaches or *modalities*. The choice of modality is often dictated by the preferred therapeutic approach of the supervisor. This can, in most instances, be useful for those supervisees who practise the same modality. Indeed, it can even be useful for those who are not familiar with that modality, in that experiencing it can lead practitioners to expand their competency in the other modality, if there is wider training in delivering therapy to service users in that modality. These modalities are distinct from supervisory models which may or may not adhere to a theoretical modality (more about models later).

Psychodynamic modality

The psychodynamic supervisory approach rests primarily on the relationship between the supervisor and supervisee. The approach can model a therapeutic process in itself, although the format of supervision adhering to this modality varies (Nelson, 2014). The supervisory relationship is akin to a therapeutic relationship, with a focus on transference and counter-transference as modes to explore the supervisee and service user relationship. The supervisory time is spent exploring relationship dynamics, which highlight areas needing development, practitioner competence, reflection and so forth.

Cognitive behavioural modality

The cognitive behavioural approach is structured and goal-oriented, more so than other modalities. There is an emphasis on teaching as well as on the cognitive restructuring of a supervisee's erroneous assumptions (Liese & Beck, 1997). Also central to this approach is an evaluation of progress towards supervisory goals. As opposed to the psychodynamic modality, a cognitive behavioural approach lends itself to the use of audio and/or video recording (James, Milne, Marie-Blackburn, & Armstrong, 2007), which can be an excellent resource upon which to base much of the activity that supervision demands.

Solution-focused modality

As in all modalities, the supervisory process mimics the process of therapy in relation to that particular modality. Marek, Sandifer, Beach, Coward and Protinsky (1994) suggest that a solution-focused approach should primarily be used in the supervision of a practitioner in solution-focused therapy training. With a focus on empowerment, supervision centres on the language and assumptions of the supervisee, the provision of support and positive reframing (Selekman & Todd, 1995). This modality adopts a more positive approach, with a focus on the supervisee's own goals and strengths (Nelson, 2014).

Person-centred modality

The focus of the person-centred modality in supervision is the belief that the supervisee has the necessary capacity to resolve practice issues and to develop therapeutic skills. The supervisor is seen as a collaborator rather than an expert, and their role is to ensure that they provide the correct environment for the practitioner to be open to their therapeutic experiences (Lambers, 2000). The quality of the supervisor–supervisee relationship is key in ensuring the success of this approach.

These modalities are only a few examples of what supervision might look like if based on a particular therapeutic model. Over time, each modality will be subject to adaptation and change, relative to the current favoured approach for that therapeutic modality. Of course, it is rarely the case that supervisor and supervisee sit down beforehand to discuss their favoured modality (if there is such an open discussion, it should be welcomed). Often, the approach to supervision will mimic the approach to therapy that the supervisor adopts. It should be noted that many texts on this topic term the therapeutic modalities described here as orientation based models, whereas I prefer to take a different view. They do not have to be exclusive. In essence, the supervision model used is the structure that informs the supervision session whereas the therapeutic modality informs the style in which that model is delivered.

Supervision Models

Supervisory models inform the structure of the supervison process. These can be developmental, i.e. where supervision aims to facilitate growth consistent with where the supervisee is in terms of their professional development, or integrated, i.e. eclectic in function combining theoretical ideas or techniques.

Developmental models of supervision

Typically, the developmental model of supervision focuses on where the supervisee is along their career trajectory, i.e. whether they are they in training, a novice, an expert, etc. Supervision aims to develop the supervisee, and it is the supervisor's responsibility (in collaboration with the supervisee) to correctly identify the supervisee's developmental stage and to support the supervisee's progression to the next stage (Stoltenberg & Delworth, 1987). The term 'scaffolding' is used in the literature to describe this process (Zimmerman & Schunk, 2003). The supervisee uses the current skills they have mastered to move on to the more advanced next stage. Central to this process is the interaction between supervisor and supervisee. Although the process appears linear, it is not. There are many aspects of a practitioner's role where mastery in one element does not necessarily mean mastery in all.

Integrated Developmental Model

The Integrated Developmental Model (IDM) proposes that there are three stages of development for the supervisee (Stoltenberg, 1981). The stages move from 'novice', which is stage 1 level, to what is termed 'master professional', which is stage 3. Trainees in the profession start at stage 1, where they are seen as displaying limited knowledge and experience and a strong motivation to learn. These individuals can also be fearful of negative evaluation. At stage 2, trainees are gaining knowledge and skills, and there are fluctuating levels of confidence and motivation. At stage 3, practitioners are secure in their knowledge and skills, displaying stable motivation and greater understanding of self. The model distinguishes between demonstrating stage 3 skills, where the practitioner is striving for autonomy, and stage 3 (integrated), where the practitioner demonstrates stage 3 skills across multiple domains, has insightful awareness and personal autonomy. According to Stoltenberg and Delworth (1987), the movement through these stages depends on the supervisee's ability for growth. In stage 1, the supervisor acts as an educator and source of knowledge as well as a source of support (to help through anxiety) and hesitancy (to promote self-efficacy). The supervisor is therefore more directive in this early stage. In stage 2, the supervisor is directive when needed, but is also able to allow the supervisee space for autonomy, and in stage 3, the supervisor provides opportunities which challenge. The focus of this particular model is firmly on the supervisor, who has the responsibility of guiding the practitioner through each stage. It focuses very much on practitioners in training and is therefore not so applicable to more experienced practitioners. The IDM approach also lacks a clear delination of process so it is difficult to tell what it might look like in practice. It also assumes that the supervisor is at the expert level, and thus emphasises a power imbalance.

Ronnestad and Skovholt's developmental model

Ronnestad and Skovholt's development model builds on the IDM through viewing the practitioner's development across their whole career (Ronnestad & Skovholt, 2003). In this model, there are six phases of development. The first three phases are similar in nature to the stages of the IDM and are termed (1) the lay helper, (2) the beginning student phase, (3) the advanced student phase, and the further phases relate to post-training development: (4) the novice professional, (5) the experienced professional and the (6) senior professional. Notably, Ronnestad and Skovholt (2003) adopted the term 'phase' instead of 'stage' so as to highlight the progressive nature of the changes in development. Ronnestad and Skovholt highlight the complex nature of practitioner development and note the influence of practitioner development on therapeutic outcomes. The task for the superviso'r in adopting this model is to remain sensitive to the supervisee's development according to the outlined phases, adapting the supervisory interventions or approach to the readiness of the supervisee.

Integrative models of supervision

Intergrative models are an eclectic collection of more than one theory and technique (Haynes, Corey, & Moulton, 2003). Haynes and colleagues describe two approaches: (1) technical eclecticism, i.e. a collection of techniques, and (2) theoretical integration, i.e. a collection of theories (ideas). An example of an integrative model of supervision is Bernard's discrimination model.

Bernard's discrimination model

According to Bernard (1979), the purpose of supervision is to produce more competent practitioners, therefore the choice of content in supervision should relate directly to skills that demonstrate competence. According to Bernard, competence involves the following: (1) process behaviours, e.g. overt behaviours such as interviewing skills and interpreting assessment information, (2) conceptualisations, e.g. covert behaviours such as identifying themes from what the service user is saying, or choosing appropriate strategies, and (3) personalisation, e.g. personal aspects such as taking responsibility for knowledge and skills, and being able to deal with challenging feedback. These three areas of learning can form the focus of supervision sessions. In addition to the purpose of supervision, Bernard outlined a second dimension which is the approach used by the supervisor. This is a deliberate choice that should be based on sound rationale. In brief, these roles are (1) teacher, (2) counsellor, and (3) consultant. Figure 3.1 shows examples of these roles in action, according to the focus of supervision.

Supervisor (focus area)	Teacher	Counsellor	Consultant
Process	Working with the practitioner to ensure they are proficient in delivering an intervention	Working through difficulites in delivering aspects of the intervention	Exploring different therapeutic styles with the practitioner
Conceptualisation	Working on formulation skills where the practitioner might have missed key areas of concern	Working on practitioner confidence in working with a service user who is avoidant	Providing information on different approaches to formulation
Personalisation	Working on identifying certain practitioner characteristics that negatively impact on therapeutic processes	Working with the practitioner to overcome avoidance of conflict in therapeutic practice	Supporting the practitioner in exploring feelings towards negative feedback

Figure 3.1   Diagrammatic represenation of Bernard's Discrimination Model

Despite there being many different approaches based on therapeutic modalities or models, it can be useful for the supervisee and supervisor (whether individually or together) to consider which approach is the best fit for their skill and experience. A wider eclectic approach may be adopted where the approaches guide the different aims and aspects of supervision.

What is presented here is not an exhaustive list; the aim is merely to inform the reader of the myriad possibilities when conducting and receiving supervision.

Challenges in Supervision

As noted in the chapter on multidisciplinary team working, professional relationships can be supportive but also challenging. It is most important to remember that supervision is *not* personal therapy.

It can be easy to fall into the trap of using supervision as a means of 'offloading' concerns and issues. There is a fine line between personal and professional development, and it is the 'personal' aspect of supervision that can be most challenging to define (Yegdich, 1999). The aim of supervision is as outlined at the beginning of this chapter, and responsibility lies with the supervisee as much as with the supervisor when personal or professional issues affect their wellbeing. According to the British Psychological Society (2014), the following challenges can occur in the supervisory relationship:

- Maintaining confidentiality – this relates to self-disclosure (when to break confidentiality, e.g. in the event of poor practice) or bringing a case to supervision without the explicit consent of the service user/supervisee.

- Safeguarding issues – dealing with safeguarding is typically covered in organisational policies, but it can be a challenge in supervision when the supervisee has not acted according to organisational policy or professional body requirements, creating a safeguarding concern.
- Whistleblowing – this is particularly challenging given the consequences for those alerting the organisation or other relevant organisations of wrong-doing, and it could directly involve the supervisee or supervisor. Such consequences can influence whether a supervisee discloses at all, and the supervisory relationship is key in allowing an open discussion of such issues (or the potential for such issues). The supervisory contract can be useful in outlining the process.
- Personal issues – this is tied in with self-disclosure, where a supervisee may open up to the supervisor about a situation that is impacting on their health and wellbeing and may therefore influence the supervisee's professional practice. If this occurs, the supervisor must be able to discuss the impact of such issues while being supportive of the supervisee's situation.
- Fitness to practise (own and others) – this can occur when personal issues impact on a supervisee's fitness to practise. There may also be concerns raised in supervision about the practice of others. It can be a sensitive issue. The supervisor must be willing to *act* on the information, whether through advising the supervisee of a way forward or via alerting more senior management to the situation. A level of judgement needs to be employed as to what is and what isn't a cause for concern.
- Capability issues – there is nothing quite so difficult as telling someone that they are not competent in one or more areas of their practice. It highlights the challenges of feedback. Such issues may be framed as learning oppor-tunities, as long as they do not impact negatively on service users.
- Ethical dilemmas (otherwise known as moral dilemmas) – they can involve challenging situations where a choice needs to be made based on accepted norms and organisational requirements. We all have our indi-vidual moral compasses, which guide our professional actions. When a supervisor has a different moral opinion from a supervisee, it can lead to challenges in supervision. Sometimes it can afford a valuable oppor-tunity for professional development (where there are no safeguarding/risk issues needing immediate action). Also, should both supervisor and supervisee hold the same opinion, it is important to reflect on the validity of this opinion.
- Boundary violations – these can involve boundaries between super-visor and supervisee, supervisee and service user, and supervisee and other members of the organisation. They can include inappropri-ate self-disclosure as well as relationship dynamics and unacceptable behaviour.

Multicultural Aspects of Supervision

Thomas (2014) asserts the importance of competence in the supervision of practitioners from different cultures. Despite there being an implicit acknowledgement of this need for cultural competence in all ethical codes and professional guidelines, literature exists highlighting the negative experiences encountered by supervisees from ethnic and culturally diverse backgrounds (e.g. Constantine, 2001). Supervision from a multicultural perspective needs to consider the impact of differences in culture and race between supervisor and supervisee explicitly, the impact of culture and race between supervisee and service user, and between members of the multidisciplinary team. These issues impact on both the supervisor's and supervisee's personal and professional development. Despite there being explicit recognition of the need to practise reflectively and to use supervision as a forum within which to do this, unless deliberate attention is given to issues of diversity, there is a danger that such discussion will not happen.

Ancis and Ladany (2001) provide a useful framework for recognising multicultural competencies in supervision. The framework encompasses the following domains: (1a) supervisor personal development, (1b) supervisee personal development (e.g. self-reflection regarding values, biases, limitations and knowledge), (2) conceptualisation (understanding the impact of individual and contextual factors on service users' lives, e.g. stereotyping and oppression), (3) intervention (the use of relevant and sensitive interventions across diverse populations), (4) process (a supervisory relationship based on respect and open communication), and (5) evaluation (recognising trainee limitation and taking remedial action). Based on these domains, factors that can increase competence and the expression of competence can be identified.

Multicultural competencies in supervision

- Acknowledging strengths and limitations of multicultural knowledge.
- Being proactive in introducing multicultural aspects into supervision.
- Acknowledging cultural biases, background, values and/or experiences.
- Being aware of the clinical impact of racism and oppression.
- Being aware of the impact of the supervisee's cultural and racial background on service users.
- Encouraging multicultural awareness.
- Acknowledging the influence of power dynamics.

All these factors can be introduced by both the supervisor and supervisee.

Diversity across age, gender, social class, religion, disability and sexual orientation need attention. Most organisations have mandatory training in equality and diversity, so it could be assumed that such matters are acknowledged,
but in practice, such recognition can often be absent. See Chapter 6 on equality and diversity for more on this topic. The impact of these issues on practice
with service users will be considered in Chapter 4 on ethical practice.

Summary

Having presented here the key elements of clinical supervision that need to be
considered, the reader should feel greater confidence in their knowledge of
clinical supervision. Ultimately, the aim of clinical supervision is to protect the
service user, ensuring that the practitioner psychologist engages in best practice, and has the skill and competency to engage in their work. Supervision is
also a place to discuss learning needs and to identify learning opportunities,
with a focus on self-awareness through practising reflectively. It can seem that
there are far too many tasks to undertake in a one-hour supervision space.
However, the elements discussed in this chapter are fluid, and need not dominate every supervision session. Supervision does not only constitute a chat
about challenging cases where guidance is sought; it should encompass all the
elements discussed in this chapter. It is a professional skill that should be part
of every practitioner psychologists' tool kit.

This chapter has covered the role of the supervisor and the role of the supervisee, while acknowledging that each practitioner will engage in both these
roles during their career. Various approaches to supervision exist, although
the traditional one-to-one format tends to be the favoured approach. Ultimately, supervision aims to cover the following key relationships: (1) supervisee and service user, (2) supervisee and supervisor, and (3) supervisee and
their professional development. Ethical practice requires that the supervisee
seek informed consent from the service user to discuss the service user's case
with their supervisor. Equally, the supervisor should seek consent from the
supervisee in discussing aspects of their supervision. The supervisee should
feel safe in bringing all aspects of their professional practice to supervision,
with explicit knowledge that they will be receiving feedback, acknowledging
deficiencies in their skills, reporting areas of poor practice or outcome. The
supervisory contract is key in supporting the relationship between supervisor
and supervisee.

Effective supervision between supervisor and supervisee involves the
development of a strong relationship, where the supervisor demonstrates that
they have the necessary clinical skill and knowledge to support the supervisee, and that both the supervisor and supervisee are open to the process and
show a keenness to engage in the supervisory process. The supervisor and
supervisee need to be flexible and available to engage in the process. Various

therapeutic modalities and supervisory models can guide supervision, but a degree of eclecticism can be helpful where 'one size fits all' is not appropriate.

Supervision can be challenging, but it is from these challenges that true learning can occur. Supervision without such challenges would be worrying, as it suggests that it is only touching on surface-level issues. Clinical supervision can sometimes be seen as being more appropriate and necessary for trainees and early career practitioners. It is not. Supervision should be a process engaged in actively throughout a career. Skills and knowledge have to adapt and change, and supervision allows the practitioner psychologist the opportunity to recognise and further develop their practice, in addition to increasing self-awareness and allowing space for reflection. At the very core of supervision is the wellbeing of the practitioner.

Key Points

- Clinical supervision is different from managerial supervision and should entail support, career development, personal development and skills development in a safe space.
- Supervisors have a responsibility to monitor the ethical practice of the supervisee.
- Effective supervisors (and supervisees) are willing to engage, flexible, accepting and available.
- A supervisory contract is essential in planning and adhering to the practical aspects of supervision.
- Self-disclosure is a key aspect of effective supervision but should be handled with care; too much self-disclosure can challenge boundaries.
- Supervision is NOT personal therapy.
- Therapeutic modalities and supervisory models can aid the practice of supervision, but an eclectic approach also works.
- Issues of diversity should be discussed in supervision, from the perspective of not only the service user, but also the practitioner.
- Supervision is a career-long endeavour; complacency can lead to adopting tried-and-tested techniques, relying on outdated skills and knowledge, and boredom.

Practice Case Studies

Case Study 1

You are an Educational Psychologist working in a child and adolescent mental health team. The team consists of a mix of professions and includes a psychiatrist, two Clinical Psychologists and a cognitive behavioural therapist. You enjoy your work and this is your first job since qualifying – you have been with the team for 12 months.

You meet with your supervisor every two weeks. Your supervisor is a senior Educational Psychologist based within your team. You often worry that your supervisor tends to focus on developmental issues, such as your confidence and therapeutic input. You also feel that the supervisor has no confidence in you but you do not know why. This is made worse as your supervisor has close relationships with other members of the team whom you are finding it difficult to get along with. You begin to question your practice, your professional integrity and your position in the team.

These factors are making you dread your supervision sessions and you find yourself losing motivation. You are concerned that this situation will negatively impact on your career progression. You have started to look at job adverts as you no longer wish to remain in your current role.

Suggested questions

1. How might you approach this situation?
2. What might have stopped this situation from developing?

Case Study 2

You have been working as a Health Psychologist for two years. You recently started working in a diabetes service in the local NHS trust. The team you work with is a mix of specialist nurses, consultant specialists and Clinical Psychologists. You feel you have settled into the team, and have developed good working relationships with your colleagues.

You are supervising a trainee Health Psychologist. During a supervision session, the trainee tells you that they are struggling to develop good working relationships with the rest of the team. They feel that they are not taken seriously when contributing in team meetings. You have been kind and empathetic, but are unsure how to help with the situation. You suspect that, professionally, the other members of the team do not value the trainee's knowledge and skills as they have not yet qualified. You also note that the trainee is withdrawn and that other members of the team have voiced concerns to you that they do not feel the trainee is fully competent in their role. You have particular concerns over the contact between a young inpatient and the trainee, where their professional relationship has veered into a friendship. You are concerned that boundaries have been crossed.

Suggested questions

1. What would be your first action be in this case?
2. Which aspects of the supervisory contract might be useful in this situation?

References

American Psychological Association. (2010). *Ethical Principles of Psychologists and Code of Conduct*. Washington, DC: APA.

Ancis, J. R., & Ladany, N. (2001). A multicultural framework for counselor supervision. In J. R. Ancis & N. Ladany (Eds.), *Counselor Supervision: Principles, Process, and Practice* (pp.63–90). New York: Brunner-Routledge.

Barnett, J. E., Erickson Cornish, J. A., Goodyear, R. K., & Lichtenberg, J. W. (2007). Commentaries on the ethical and effective practice of clinical supervision. *Professional Psychology: Research and Practice, 38*(3), 268a.

Bernard, J. M. (1979). Supervisor training: A discrimination model. *Counselor Education and Supervision, 19*(1), 60–68.

British Psychological Society. (2009). *Code of Ethics and Conduct*. Leicester: BPS.

British Psychological Society. (2014). *Code of Human Research Ethics*. Leicester: BPS. Retrieved from www.bps.org.uk/sites/www.bps.org.uk/files/Policy/Policy%20-%20 Files BPS%20Code%20of%20Human%20Research%20Ethics.pdf

Clevinger, K., Albert, E., & Raiche, E. (2019). Supervisor self-disclosure: Supervisees' perceptions of positive supervision experiences. *Training and Education in Professional Psychology, 13*(3), 222–226. https://doi.org/10.1037/tep0000236

Constantine, M. G. (2001). Perspectives on multicultural supervision. *Journal of Multicultural Counseling and Development, 29*(2), 98–98.

Haynes, R., Corey, G., & Moulton, P. (2003). *Clinical Supervision in the Helping Professions: A Practical Guide*. Pacific Grove, CA: Brooks/Cole.

Howgego, I. M., Yellowlees, P., Owen, C., Meldrum, L., & Dark, F. (2003). The therapeutic alliance: The key to effective patient outcome? A descriptive review of the evidence in community mental health case management. *Australian and New Zealand Journal of Psychiatry, 37*(2), 169–183.

James, I. A., Milne, D., Marie-Blackburn, I., & Armstrong, P. (2007). Conducting successful supervision: Novel elements towards an integrative approach. *Behavioural and Cognitive Psychotherapy, 35*, 191.

Ladany, N., Ellis, M. V., & Friedlander, M. L. (1999). The supervisory working alliance, trainee self-efficacy, and satisfaction with supervision. *Journal of Counseling and Development, 77*, 447–455.

Ladany, N., & Lehrman-Waterman, D. E. (1999). The content and frequency of supervisor self-disclosures and their relationship to supervisor style and the supervisory working alliance. *Counselor Education and Supervision, 38*, 143–160.

Ladany, N., Mori, Y., & Mehr, K. E. (2013). Effective and ineffective supervision. *The Counseling Psychologist, 41*(1), 28–47.

Lambers, E. (2000). Supervision in person-centered therapy: Facilitating congruence. In E. Mearns & B. Thorne (Eds.), *Person-centered Therapy Today: New Frontiers in Theory and Practice* (pp. 196–211). London: Sage.

Liese, B. S., & Beck, J. S. (1997). Cognitive therapy supervision. In C. E. Watkins (Ed.), *Handbook of Psychotherapy Supervision* (pp. 114–133). Hoboken, NJ: John Wiley & Sons.

Lowry, J. L. (2001, August). Successful supervision: Supervisor and supervisee characteristics. In J. E. Barnett (Chair), *Secrets of Successful Supervision: Clinical and Ethical Issues*. Symposium conducted at the 109th Annual Convention of the American Psychological Association, San Francisco, CA.

Luepker, E. T. (2012). *Record Keeping in Psychotherapy and Counseling: Protecting Confidentiality and the Professional Relationship* (2nd ed.). New York: Routledge.

Marek, L. I., Sandifer, D. M., Beach, A., Coward, R. L., & Protinsky, H. O. (1994). Supervision without the problem. *Journal of Family Psychotherapy, 5,* 57–64.

Milne, D. (2007). An empirical definition of clinical supervision. *British Journal of Clinical Psychology, 46*(4), 437–447.

Nelson, M. L. (2014). Using the major formats of clinical supervision. In C. E. Watkins & D. C. Milne (Eds.), *The Wiley International Handbook of Clinical Supervision* (pp.308–328). Chichester: John Wiley & Sons.

Ronnestad, M. H., & Skovholt, T. M. (2003). The journey of the counselor and therapist: Research findings and perspectives on professional development. *Journal of Career Development, 30,* 5–44.

Selekman, M. D., & Todd, T. C. (1995). Co-creating a context for change in the supervisory system: The solution-focused supervision model. *Journal of Systemic Therapies, 14*(3), 21–33.

Stoltenberg, C. (1981). Approaching supervision from a developmental perspective: The counselor complexity model. *Journal of Counseling Psychology, 28*(1), 59.

Stoltenberg, C., & Delworth, U. (1987). *Supervising Counselors and Therapists: A Developmental Approach* (Jossey-Bass social and behavioral science series). San Francisco, CA: Jossey-Bass.

Thomas, J. T. (2010). *The Ethics of Supervision and Consultation: Practical Guidance for Mental Health Professionals.* Washington, D.C.: American Psychological Association.

Wulf, J., & Nelson, M. L. (2000). Experienced psychologists' recollections of internship supervision and its contributions to their development. *Clinical Supervisor, 19,* 123–145.

Yegdich, T. (1999). Lost in the crucible of supportive clinical supervision: Supervision is not therapy. *Journal of Advanced Nursing, 29*(5), 1265–1275.

Zimmerman, B. J., & Schunk, D. S. (Eds.). (2003). *Educational Psychology: A Century of Contributions.* Mahwah, NJ: Lawrence Erlbaum Associates.

4

Ethical Practice

On reading this chapter you will:

- Understand the difference between British Psychological Society guidelines and Health and Care Professions Council regulations
- Understand the complexity of ethical decision making in both practice and research
- Appreciate the need for confidentiality and under what circumstances confidentiality can be broken
- Understand the need for fully informed consent with children and adults with and without capacity
- Be aware of information governance and what it means for the practitioner
- Be aware of the risk of competing relationship roles and the importance of having clear boundaries in practice

Introduction

Professional codes of ethics

The practitioner psychologist is guided by many codes, standards and guides related to conduct. The principles of these codes guide ethical practice and can offer a framework within which the psychologist can practise. In this chapter, we will discuss the various professional codes (those available at the time of writing), but these documents will not tell the practitioner what to do; they merely serve as a guide, which must then be translated into ethical behaviour. You should also remember that many decisions are made in the moment, which means familiarity of the most up-to-date and relevant ethical codes of conduct is essential. Ultimately, ethical practice depends on reasonable judgement so that the decisions reached are in the best interest of the service user and community. In this chapter, we will discuss the professional codes of the Health and Care Professions Council and the British Psychological Society.

Health and Care Professions Council

The Health and Care Professions Council (HCPC) regulates the practice of a range of health professionals and has been set up to protect the public. It ensures that the practitioners they regulate meet the standards they lay out for professional skills (Health and Care Professions Council, 2016). The HCPC will remove practitioners from the register if they do not adhere to its codes of conduct. To be employed as a practitioner psychologist in the UK, you need to be registered with the HCPC, and it is illegal to use a protected title (e.g. Clinical Psychologist, Educational Psychologist, Health Psychologist) if you are not registered. The standards are easily accessible and available to service users, carers and the general public so that they know what to expect of the practitioners they work with. The standards advise registrants that they must familiarise themselves with the code, and on registering with the HCPC, practitioners must sign a declaration confirming they will adhere to the code. The code states that the registrant *must* observe the following standards (HCPC, 2016: 1). They demand that practitioners:

- Promote and protect the interests of service users and carers
- Communicate appropriately and effectively
- Work within the limits of their knowledge and skills
- Delegate appropriately
- Respect confidentiality
- Manage risk
- Report concerns about safety
- Be open when things go wrong
- Be honest and trustworthy
- Keep records of their work.

If these standards are not followed, the fitness to practise of the psychologist will be questioned. Should a member of the public raise a concern, the HCPC will consider whether to take action. Information on how concerns are dealt with by the HCPC can be found at www.hcpc-uk.org.

British Psychological Society

While it is the HCPC that regulates practitioner psychologists' practice and behaviour, the British Psychological Society (BPS) promotes ethical behaviour among its members. Its *Code of Ethics and Conduct* provides a framework that guides the practitioner in making ethical judgements (British Psychological Society, 2018). The BPS also governs the conduct of its members but does not determine fitness to practise. The BPS code should be used in conjunction with the *Code of Human Research Ethics* (BPS, 2014) and *Practice Guidelines* (BPS, 2017). The BPS codes and guidelines use the term 'should' rather than 'must' to emphasise their advisory nature. The BPS *Code of Ethics and Conduct* (BPS, 2018) is based on four ethical principles, each of which is described in the form of values that are based on fundamental beliefs that guide ethical decisions and acts. The principles are:

- Respect
- Competence
- Responsibility
- Integrity.

The reader will note that these principles are similar to the HCPC standards. The *Practice Guidelines* (BPS, 2017) are a source of information for practitioner psychologists that can support the ethical codes of conduct. The guidelines define what is good practice for all practitioner psychologists and covers the different contexts in which psychologists practise as well as the range of service users and their needs. The guidelines also list current legal statutes governing health and social care practice, which is extremely useful in keeping up to date with documents related to capacity, such as the Mental Capacity Act 2005 (Department of Health, 2005). The BPS *Code of Human Research Ethics* (BPS, 2014) is also an important set of guidelines for practitioner psychologists, and is discussed later in this chapter.

Professional codes and guidelines are not updated regularly, so while the information outlined here is current now, it will at some point become outdated. The central message is that practitioner psychologists are governed by different codes, guidance and legal standards. They should not only be aware of what these are and where to find them, they should also keep up to date with them as they change.

Boundaries

Although there are many ethical issues that face the practitioner psychologist, one of the most complex is that of professional boundaries. According to Knapp and Slattery (2004), the purpose of professional boundaries is to protect the service user and ensure structure and safety. The practitioner can hold multiple roles within the organisation, such as therapist, clinical supervisor, employer and researcher, but they also have roles outside the organisation, within personal, social and business settings (Sonne, 1994). Potential ethical issues arise when relationship boundaries are crossed. Sonne (1994: 338) highlights the dynamic need for emotional involvement between the practitioner and service user: 'feeling cared for, listened to, understood, and helped can lead to a sense of emotional attachment for the service user'. But practitioners need to be aware and constantly vigilant of the boundary between appropriate emotional attachment and innapropriate relationships. Although some areas are absolutely clear, e.g. sexual relationships with service users is an abuse of the therapeutic relationship, there are many areas that are not explicitly well-defined, such as the appropriateness of accepting gifts, self-disclosure and hugging service users (Knapp & Slattery, 2004).

Boundary setting, both within and beyond the therapy room, is covered in the BPS *Practice Guidelines* (2017), where the focus is on balancing good relationships and trust within specific boundaries. The guidelines refer to keeping an emotional distance from service users, carers and relatives and that maintaining this is part of the practitioners duty of care, even after the professional relationship has ended. Practitioners should avoid being in a multiple relationship with a service user, but in a situation where no other practitioner with the required expertise is available, then the practitioner psychologist must maintain objectivity, alert their manager and clinical supervisor, and make a note in service user's records stating what the relationship is.

Maintaining appropriate boundaries is also mentioned in the HCPC *Standards of Conduct* (2016), although here it merely states that relationships with service users and carers should remain professional.

Boundary issues are clearly complex and the practitioner is advised to seek support from a clinical supervisor should such issues present themselves in practice.

Competence

Here, 'competence' refers to professional competence, as opposed to service user competence, which will be discussed later in this chapter in relation to informed consent. It is the responsibility of the psychologist to ensure that they are competent in their practice and that they are able to recognise the limits of their skills and experience. Professional competency is covered in the BPS *Code of Ethics and Conduct* (2018) and the HCPC *Standards of Proficiency for Practitioner Psychologists* (2015). Competence is one of the core ethical principles of the BPS *Code of Ethics and Conduct* and is described as 'working within the recognised limits of their knowledge, skill, training, education and experience' (BPS, 2018: 6). The values underpinning this principle are primarily skills-based and include competence in communicating and relating to others, advancing the evidence base, and the ability to make decisions based on professional ethics. The HCPC *Standards of Proficiency* (2015) cover areas of competence in detail, and it is these areas that should be the focus of supervision, continuing professional development and training.

Clinical supervision

Once qualified, the practitioner psychologist should engage in supervision, which in part is to ensure that the practitioner is working within their competence (for the safety of the service user). It is in supervision that both supervisor and supervisee can identify areas where further training or support is needed. This is one of the most important aspects of supervision and is an ethical requirement of the supervisor; that is, the supervisor should be competent to supervise and monitor the competence of the supervisee. Vasquez (1992) emphasises that psychologists who supervise should have the necessary knowledge and skills of practice, which are acquired through training or supervised experience. For more information on supervisory skills, see Chapter 3 on supervision.

Science-informed competency

Bieschke, Foult, Collins and Halonen (2004) highlight the importance of science-informed competency. While Chapter 1 on evidence-based practice covers the required skills of the scientist-practitioner, practitioner competence requires an ability to address relevant research questions and to apply research methods in general. In accordance with the BPS *Code of Ethics and Conduct* (2018), the practitioner psychologist should be aware of advances in the evidence base, implying that familiarisation with and the consumption of the latest research in the area of practice is essential. Bieschke and colleagues stipulate the following components of science-informed practice for the practitioner psychologist:

- Finding and applying current research knowledge and theory to practice.
- Contributing to the knowledge base.
- Adopting a critical approach to reported outcomes of interventions.
- Taking a more socio-cultural stance on how research is conducted.
- Accessing external networks (e.g. stakeholders, including service users) with regard to the conduct and practice of science.

The scientifically informed psychologist is also required to adopt the same skillset as a scientist when conducting assessments and in formulating a service user's difficulties. The assessment is a systematic approach to gathering data which informs the formulation and intervention. Having a thorough knowledge of the theoretical basis of the measures used, their validity and generalisability, their cultural validity and their use with a particular service user group necessitates adopting the same scientific methods that a researcher might use. The manipulation of data from a variety of sources and its conceptualisation are skills that develop from research practice. Thus, the skills of the scientist and of the practitioner inform competence in practice.

Confidentiality

The expectation is that within the therapy space, all information shared with the practitioner psychologist is confidential. The practitioner has a duty to ensure this confidentiality. However, that being said, there are limitations. When initially setting up the therapy contract, it is essential that the practitioner clearly communicates when confidentiality may need to be broken. An example is when a general practitioner (GP) may need to be contacted if a service user displays self-harming behaviours or talks about suicide, or there may be safeguarding issues if the service user's behaviour presents a danger to others and it is then in the public interest to prevent such actions (Tribe & Morrissey, 2020). Within the area of forensic psychology, in particular, there are obvious limitations of confidentiality. Tribe and Morrissey (2020) use the example of the Egdell case, when the psychiatrist of a prisoner who was seeking early release broke his service user's confidentiality to alert the relevant authorities of the substantial risk he posed to the public. Despite legal action being taken against the psychiatrist for breaking confidentiality, the psychiatrist successfully defended their decision because it was in the public interest to do so. The issue around matters of public interest is that it is assumed; it cannot be known for sure. The practitioner can only express a view based on their knowledge, skills and expertise. The practitioner should therefore be careful to take action only after seeking and following appropriate legal advice.

Within the initial meeting with a new service user, then, it is important that the practitioner sets out what those limits to confidentiality are, and under what circumstances they are required to break that confidentiality. It is important to make the distinction between seeking informed consent from the service user to disclose information in clinical supervision, peer reflection or within the context of multidisciplinary team meetings, when it is also necessary to gain service user consent, and circumstances where this might not apply or where this might not be possible. Such circumstances include the risk of harm to the service user or to others (as a result of the service user's actions or the actions of others), with or without legal or safeguarding implications.

Complications can arise from situations where such disclosure may result in serious harm to the service user. For example, an area of conflict for the practitioner is when there might be the need to report allegations of child abuse (when the service user discloses information about a potential perpetrator, or their own actions or when they have been abused in the past). There is no mandatory legal requirement (England and Wales) for the practitioner psychologist to disclose abuse to the relevant authorities, although there will be child protection guidelines as part of a contract of employment.

It is morally and ethically challenging to consider that there may be situations where breaching confidentiality in potential child abuse cases may not be appropriate. However, to illustrate such complexity, consider a case where there may be allegations of historical abuse which the service user does not want the practitioner to pursue further, due to the service user's perceived fear of losing their family (if the perpetrator is a family member) or of not being believed. Should such disclosure happen without the service user's consent, this can have a severe impact on the service user's relationship with the practitioner, the continued therapeutic provision and current risk (e.g. self-harm or suicidal ideation). The practitioner psychologist must therefore weigh up the benefits and harms of such a breach in confidentiality.

Decisions where it might be necessary to breach confidentiality are challenging, and the practitioner should be familiar with local guidance, legal implications and organisational policy. Of course, these don't tell the practitioner how to weigh up such complex decisions; responsibility lies with the practitioner psychologist. However, in its *Practice Guidelines*, the BPS suggests some organisational sources of guidance (BPS, 2017):

- The Information Governance team (see below)
- The data/clinical governance department/lead
- The safeguarding team
- Legal departments.

Confidentiality with young people

Knowledge of confidentiality practice when working with young people is crucial. The principles of 'Gillick competence' or the 'Fraser guidelines' are key, and the wishes of the young person should take precedence over the need for disclosure to interested parties such as parents, guardians, social workers, etc., unless there are safeguarding issues. The principles of 'Gillick competence' stem from a legal case in the 1980s when a young person, under the age of 16, sought contraception without parental consent. It was determined that if a young person under the age of 16 demonstrates the maturity to make a decision, they should be able to do so in confidence. The 'Fraser guidelines' tend to dominate the medical field, whereas in therapeutic practice, it is 'Gillick competence' that is most often quoted. Individuals with parental responsibility do not have an automatic right to such confidential information, and a young person deemed to be Gillick competent is able to work with the practitioner psychologist independently.

Information Governance

'Information Governance' is the term used to cover the policies, procedures, accountability and management structures within health and social care organisations for the creation, storage, use and destruction of information. This includes personal information and personal identifiable information. The Data Protection Act 2018 is a legal act outlining the UK's response to the General Data Protection Regulation (GDPR). According to the Act, those responsible for using personal data must adhere to the rules of 'data protection principles'. These state that information should be:

- Used legally and transparently
- Used for a specific purpose
- Used only for what is necessary
- Accurate and up to date
- Kept no longer than appropriate
- Kept securely.

Although health and social care organisations will have their own policies and procedures relating to the principles of GDPR, practitioner psychologists need to be aware of how this impacts on confidentiality and record keeping, especially the management and creation of service user notes. The BPS *Practice Guidelines* (2017) includes a comprehensive discussion of all aspects of confidentiality. The reader needs to be familiar with the guidelines. In brief, all records relating to a service user can be accessed by the service user (they have a legal right to access these records), practice managers and those involved in the care of the service user. Record-keeping therefore needs to be balanced between fact and subjective opinion. All service user records (whether paper or electronic records) have to be kept secure. The practitioner is reminded that this includes not only direct work with the service user, but also any work concerning the organisation and other involved parties. Record-keeping is a skill that is developed over time. On qualifying (or in training), it is typical for the novice to write copious notes in case they miss an important fact. Of course, this means that anyone reading the notes has an arduous task ahead of them to identify the salient points. So, practitioner psychologists need to learn to be concise and to the point in their note taking.

Guidelines on note-taking

According to the BPS *Practice Guidelines* (2017), the following rules should be kept in mind when taking notes:

- Notes should be easy to follow, sufficiently detailed but concise.
- Language needs to be accessible.
- Notes need to be accurate.
- Notes need to be kept up to date – it is easy to fall behind in note keeping so ensure there is enough time after each service user contact to write up your notes.
- Notes need to be relevant.

How long should records be kept?

The BPS *Practice Guidelines* (2017) suggest that a practitioner psychologist's records should be kept for as long as required, and in accordance with legal, national and local policy processes. For those in private practice, the general guide is a period of seven years. Records should be destroyed in a manner that is consistent with organisational policies or, if the practitioner is in private practice, through the use of industry-standard destruction services.

Informed Consent

According to the *Practice Guidelines* (BPS, 2017), it is stated that informed consent should be obtained without influence and given freely. It is embedded in the idea that service users are able to choose whether to engage in therapy or psychological assessment and subsequent intervention. The important term here is of course 'informed', and it is the aim of this section to consider what 'informed' looks like in practice.

The process needs to fit the purpose for which consent is sought and such consent should be reviewed regularly. Here lies the potential for bias, and the practitioner should check in with their own values and their wish to help. There is the potential for a power imbalance and assumption of freely given consent when such consent is due to the service user's malleability or wish to please. The message given by the BPS guidelines is that such consent should be monitored regularly.

To make an informed choice service users need a full account of the potential benefits but also of the potential harm that may be caused by an assessment, intervention or other psychological treatment. In a national survey undertaken by Crawford and colleagues (2016), data drawn from a sample across England and Wales showed that many service users reported lasting negative effects from psychological treatment. The study concluded that participants were less likely to report lasting negative effects if they felt they had been adequately informed about the treatment they received beforehand.

Guidelines on gaining informed consent

The BPS *Practice Guidelines* (2017) suggest the following need to be covered in gaining informed consent:

- A description of what is involved in the work that will be engaged in.
- The benefits and risks of engaging in the work.
- The risks and benefits of not engaging in the work.

- Any alternative methods that could be used (and the benefits and risks of these methods).
- The potential to feel worse before things improve in therapy.
- That the service user has the right to withdraw consent at any stage.

Confidentiality, and specifically the limits of confidentiality, also need to be clearly communicated to the service user.

Capacity to Consent

It is probable that a practitioner psychologist will at some point encounter a situation where they are working with individuals who lack capacity to consent. According to the BPS document *What Makes a Good Capacity Assessment* (2019), all HCPC-registered psychologists can complete competency assessments within the boundaries laid out by the Mental Capacity Act 2005 (MCA; Department of Health, 2005). The capacity to consent can be affected by a range of factors, such as cognitive ability (intellectual disability, dementia, brain injury) or a severe mental health condition. The MCA is designed to promote the rights of individuals who lack capacity and is used to guide action and any capacity assessment relevant to a specific decision. What is inherent in the MCA is the need for the service user to have the support and information (in adapted formats if necessary) and the time they need in order to be part of the decision-making process. The lack of capacity to make an informed decision in one area of life does not mean the individual does not have capacity to make other decisions. It is also important to keep in mind that capacity for a specific decision may fluctuate over time.

The Mental Capacity Act 2005

The MCA (Department of Health, 2005) outlines the following principles that should guide those considering whether an individual has capacity:

- That the service user has capacity unless proven otherwise.
- That the service user should be supported to make their own decisions.
- That it is OK for the service user to make a decision that others may feel is unwise.
- That any decisions made on behalf of an individual who lacks capacity should be in their best interest.
- The least restrictive action should be taken, depending on the circumstances of the situation.

How to assess capacity to consent

The MCA asks that where there is a query about an individual's capacity, the following two-stage test is required:

1. Is there an impairment of mind or brain as a result of illness or factors such as alcohol or drug use?
2. Does the impairment mean that the individual is unable to make a specific decision, at that time?

For stage 1, a formal diagnosis is not required, but if there are questions about whether a service user's symptoms meet the first stage of the two-stage test, a multidisciplinary approach should be taken (BPS, 2019). For stage 2, it is the assessment of function that determines whether an individual is able to make a decision (see below).

According to the MCA, an individual is able to make a decision if they can:

*   Understand the information that relates to that specific decision.
*   Retain that information.
*   Weigh up the risks and benefits of making that decision.

It is always necessary to ensure that the service user has the support they need in order to be able to indicate their understanding and their consent. For example, a pictorial version of a verbal description of what will happen in therapy can be used. Also consider whether there is a family member or carer who can help with establishing consent and capacity. It might be appropriate to delay any decision to a time of day when the individual has better cognitive capabilities. It is important to note that, under the MCA, all health and social care practitioners are duty-bound to adopt its principles (this applies to practitioners in private practice also). For more complex capacity issues, such as power of attorney, there is further information in the BPS *Practice Guidelines* (2017). The BPS guide *What Makes a Good Capacity Assessment* (BPS, 2019), which has everything the practitioner psychologist needs (including case examples) when conducting a capacity assessment, is also a useful resource.

Research Ethics

The BPS's *Code of Human Research Ethics* (2014), which has informed many institutional policies related to research with human participants, is the key resource on research ethics. Participants in psychological research need to be assured of their safety and the appropriateness of the research when placing their trust in the research investigators. Although guidelines exist, such as the BPS's *Code*, it is still the judgement of the practitioner/researcher that determines the process of research and the ethical principles therein.

The principles of conducting ethical research

The core principles of conducting ethical research, as outlined by the BPS *Code of Human Research Ethics* (2014), are as follows:

- The scientific rationale.
- Social responsibility.
- The risk–benefit rationale.
- Ensuring the autonomy, privacy and dignity of participants.

Risk

Risk relates to either physical or psychological harm. It includes the potential distress or discomfort that may result from the research process or procedures. Although it is challenging to consider all the potential risks (some risks only become apparent while conducting the research), there should be measures in place to ensure that there is a process to follow should such risks become apparent. Ethical review bodies do require that there is a safety protocol in place prior to the commencement of research. The more complex risk issues arise when there may be capacity concerns, or if the participant is a child. The research may involve sensitive topics, such as self-harm, abuse or violence, which may act as triggers for the participant. The need for deception, access to confidential information, painful or uncomfortable procedures (filling in questionnaires for a significant length of time can be uncomfortable) and biological testing are just a few areas where risk must be considered.

Capacity to consent in research

In a similar way to gaining consent in therapeutic settings, every person who contributes data for research should freely give their consent. This includes consent to agree to the procurement of that data, and to be able to withdraw from the research at any time without penalty, and to withdraw any data that they have already contributed. The BPS *Code of Human Research Ethics* (2014) suggests that the methods of gaining consent are proportional to the participant's role and the potential risk of harm. There is a vast difference in accessing data from a database where the participant has already consented to that data being used for research purposes and whose data has been anonymised, and a research study that explores the nature and significance of sexual consent in victims of rape through directly interviewing survivors of rape.

Children under the age of 16

Where a child under the age of 16 is deemed competent (see the earlier section on 'Gillick competence'), they are able to provide consent without the involvement of parents or guardians should they choose (although it is always good practice to involve the parents or guardians). In assessing the competence of the child, the following guidelines should be followed:

- The child should be provided with information about the study, in language appropriate to their age and needs.
- This information should be provided by individuals with experience of working with children.
- The researcher needs to consider the wishes of the child, e.g. a refusal to take part or to withdraw from the study should be accepted.
- Signing an assent form is not suitable for under 5s, but is necessary when including children between the ages of 5 and 16 years in research.
- Consent to take part in reseach needs to be continually monitored.

Persons lacking capacity

For individuals over the age of 16 years in England and Wales, the Mental Capacity Act 2005 will apply (see the section above on Capacity to Consent). Where the individual is unable to consent to taking part in research, a consultee should be appointed. The consultee is a person who:

- Is caring for the individual and/or interested in their welfare (not a paid or professional carer).
- Is willing to be consulted.

Where no appropriate consultee can be identified, a nominated consultee should be appointed in accordance with Department of Health guidance:

The role of a consultee is to voice what they believe the participant would want to do if they had capacity to consent. It is important to remember that the consultee does not give consent, but advises on what they think the participant would want. Further advice on consultee appointment can be found on the Health Research Authority website (hra.nhs.uk).

The approval of a research ethics committee is needed for research with people who lack capacity. The following requirements need to be complied with:

- The research should be focused on the impairing condition that is affecting the participant.
- The research cannot be carried out to the same effectiveness with individuals who have capacity.

- The research should balance the benefits and risks to the participant or be of benefit to the treatment and care of those with a similar condition. There should be minimal risk for research participants.
- The research should comply with section 32 (consultee) and section 33 (the right to withdraw and the right to refuse participation unless this is to protect the individual from harm) of the MCA.

Research Ethics Committees

A research ethics committee consists of volunteers who come from a range of backgrounds whose task is to formally review research proposals to determine if the research is ethical. According to the BPS *Code of Human Research Ethics* (2014), research ethics committees should adhere to a set of principles. These are that research ethics committees are:

- Independent – there should be no conflict of interest between the review body and researcher.
- Competent – research protocols should have an informed evaluation.
- Informed – there should be an understanding of what is and what is not ethical practice.
- Transparent and accountable.

There are two main types of research ethics committee. The first is within the NHS, and the second is external to the NHS, such as at a university or other type of organisation. Advice for research ethics committees outside the NHS is covered by the Economic and Social Research Council (ESRC; esrc.ukri.org).

Research within the NHS

Where the devolved administrations (in the UK) and Health Research Authority provide a research ethics service, the committees are made up of members of the public and a range of experts. These types of research ethics committee are only concerned with research that involves the following:

- Research participants who are identified in the context of their current or past use of NHS services.
- Relatives or carers of such participants.
- Previously collected human tissue.
- Access to confidential information.
- Current collections of confidential information or human tissue from such participants.

There are other requirements that need to be considered, and the reader is advised to access the 2020 edition of *Governance Arrangements for Research Ethics Committees*, which covers all devolved nations within the UK (Health Research Authority, 2021). This is currently held on the hra/nhs/uk website (as will be updated versions of the document).

Summary

This was a particularly challenging chapter to write, in part due to the complexity of ethics in practice and in part because it is impossible to cover all elements that are relevant for practitioner psychologists. The concluding statement within the BPS *Code of Ethics and Conduct* (2018: 8) sums up the difficulty:

> This Code cannot and does not aim to provide the answer to every ethical decision a Psychologist may face. The Code provides the parameters within which professional judgements should be made. However, it is important to remember to reflect and apply a process to resolve ethical challenges.

Ultimately, it lays the choice of action on the practitioner, and I believe it should. With adequate clinical supervision, professional development and reflective practice, the practitioner psychologist has the necessary tools and support to make the most informed decision. Although there may be 'best practice' protocols in certain situations, they are not always so clear in other domains. Keeping an open mind and being comfortable with accepting such challenges can be the most useful approach.

There are many codes of ethics and guidelines available that support the practitioner psychologist when they are faced with ethical issues. Whereas the BPS supports the clinician with recommendations, the HCPC holds principles that should always be upheld. Non-adherence of these principles can result in the practitioner psychologist losing their professional title and ability to practise. Where there may be difficulty is in balancing issues such as 'respecting confidentiality' and 'managing risk'. The guiding principle in both the BPS and HCPC documents relating to ethics and conduct is that of 'competence' and the ultimate goal is to protect the service user.

Confidentiality is a key concern when working in health and social care and is particularly salient in the therapy space. Breaking confidentiality is sometimes necessary, and the practitioner should be familiar with situations where this has to happen. At the very least, the service user should be fully informed of such situations and understand the potential outcomes.

One of the more complex areas is capacity to consent, and the practitioner psychologist should ensure they are informed of the legal processes to achieve consent within the therapy room and in conducting research. One of the more frequent ethical violations concerns boundaries between professional and external relationships. Although such situations are sometimes inevitable, it is important to be transparent and to seek advice.

Research ethics are as important as ethics in a therapeutic setting. The scientist-practitioner should be aware of the governance of ethical approvals from the necessary organisations. Information governance is also a key concern in both practice and research, and careful note taking and the maintenance of confidential records is essential. Ultimately, it is the practitioner psychologist who makes these key decisions, and regardless of the numerous guidelines available, practitioners must be able to justify their decisions and actions.

Key Points

- Ethical practice relates to both therapy and research.
- Ethical practice includes all areas of practice, where practitioners need to be aware of the impact of their practice and competence on others in addition to key considerations around confidentiality, informed consent and mental capacity.
- Clinical supervision, reflective practice and effective multidisciplinary team working aids the practitioner when considering ethical challenges in practice.
- Confidentiality can be broken in certain circumstances, and the service user/ research participant must be made aware of this before consenting to treatment/ research participation.
- The documents and guidelines mentioned in this chapter will be updated and changed over time, so the practitioner should always check the current guidelines.
- Guidelines and good practice documents may help to guide the practitioner, but it is the judgement of the practitioner psychologist which informs ethical decision making.

Practice Case Studies

Case Study 1

You are a Clinical Psychologist working in an adult mental health team. You have been working in this setting for a number of years and enjoy your work. You have a varied case load, and you have been working with some service users for a number of months. One of these service users has presented you with an ethical dilemma.

Jane is in her mid-20s and you have been working with her on issues related to difficulties in relationships and fear of abandonment. You feel that your work with Jane has stalled, and despite discussing this in clinical supervision, the situation persists. While concerned, you also feel that Jane is still in need of therapeutic support and you have accepted the fact that this will be a long-term piece of work.

After a period of unemployment, Jane has found a job as a marketing executive at a large organisation. Jane has begun to mention a manager within the organisation who has been exceptionally friendly towards her, making her feel uncomfortable. You know the person that she has been referring to socially and made a passing comment when Jane first mentioned him that you knew him and that he was a really nice person. Jane is now asking you questions about her manager that you feel go beyond the boundaries of the therapeutic setting. You also feel uncomfortable that the person in question has made a passing comment about 'a new girl' who has started working with him.

Suggested questions

1. What are the primary ethical issues in this case study?
2. How might the Clinical Psychologist overcome these issues while protecting the needs of the service user and re-instating professional boundaries?

Case Study 2

As a Forensic Psychologist, you have a challenging role within a prison setting. You mainly work in the rehabilitation of sex offenders and with interventions related to violence and aggression. Much of your day-to-day work involves one-to-one sessions with individual prisoners, providing assessments of risk and threat to the community, which inform court proceedings. Your notes are used as evidence, so the normal right to confidentiality does not apply.

You feel you have a good rapport with your service users and find helping them through the criminal justice system rewarding, despite your own feelings towards the crimes committed by some. You believe strongly that the principle of respect is paramount in your approach to your work, and feel that this protects your ability to maintain a professional boundary and a non-judgemental stance.

You have recently begun working with a service user who has been charged with sexual assault. They disclose to you that there is more that has happened but refuse to give you any more details until you promise them confidentiality. You are unsure whether what they are keeping from you is important information for the criminal case against them or whether it is a personal issue and unrelated to the criminal case.

You know that it is not appropriate to say that you can keep this information confidential, but you also feel that what is being withheld is an essential factor in your assessment, formulation and intervention.

Suggested questions

1. What ethical principles apply to this case?
2. What guidelines or support might be relevant here to help you?

References

Bieschke, K. J., Fouad, N. A., Collins Jr, F. L., & Halonen, J. S. (2004). The scientifically-minded psychologist: Science as a core competency. *Journal of Clinical Psychology*, *60*(7), 713–723.

British Psychological Society. (2014). *Code of Human Research Ethics*. Leicester: BPS. Retrieved from www.bps.org.uk/sites/www.bps.org.uk/files/Policy/Policy%20-%20 Files BPS%20Code%20of%20Human%20Research%20Ethics.pdf

British Psychological Society. (2017). *Practice Guidelines*. Leicester: BPS. Retrieved from www.bps.org.uk/sites/www.bps.org.uk/files/Policy/Policy%20-%20Files/ BPS%20Practice%20Guidelines%20%28Third%20Edition%29.pdf

British Psychological Society. (2018). *Code of Ethics and Conduct*. Leicester: BPS. Retrieved from www.bps.org.uk/sites/www.bps.org.uk/files/Policy/Policy%20-%20 Files/Code%20of%20Ethics%20and%20Conduct%20%282009%29.pdf

British Psychological Society. (2019). *What Makes a Good Assessment of Capacity*. Leicester: BPS. Retrieved from www.bps.org.uk/sites/www.bps.org.uk/files/Policy/ Policy%20-%20Files/What%20makes%20a%20good%20assessment%20of%20 capacity.pdf

Crawford, M., Thana, L., Farquharson, L., Palmer, L., Hancock, E., Bassett, P., ... Parry, G. (2016). Patient experience of negative effects of psychological treatment: Results of a national survey. *British Journal of Psychiatry*, *208*(3), 260–265. doi:10.1192/ bjp.bp.114.162628

Data Protection Act. (2018). London: HMSO.

Department of Health. (2005). *Mental Capacity Act (2005)*. London: HMSO.

Health and Care Professions Council. (2015). *The Standards of Proficiency for Practitioner Psychologists*. London: HCPC. Retrieved from www.hcpc-uk.org/ standards/standards-of-proficiency/practitioner-psychologists/

Health and Care Professions Council. (2016). *Standards of Conduct, Performance and Ethics*. London: HCPC. Retrieved from www.hcpc-uk.org/standards/standards-of-conduct-performance-and-ethics/

Health Research Authority. (2021) *Governance Arrangements for Research Ethics Committees*. Retrieved from https://www.hra.nhs.uk/planning-and-improving-research/policies-standards-legislation/governance-arrangement-research-ethics-committees/

Knapp, S. & Slattery, J. M. (2004). Professional boundaries in nontraditional settings. *Professional Psychology: Research and Practice*, *35*(5), 553.

Sonne, J. L. (1994). Multiple relationships: Does the new ethics code answer the right questions? *Professional Psychology: Research and Practice*, *25*(4), 336–343. https:// doi.org/10.1037/0735-7028.25.4.336

Tribe, R., & Morrissey, J. (Eds.). (2020). *The Handbook of Professional Ethical and Research Practice for Psychologists, Counsellors, Psychotherapists and Psychiatrists*. Abingdon: Routledge.

Vasquez, M. J. (1992). Psychologist as clinical supervisor: Promoting ethical practice. *Professional Psychology: Research and Practice*, *23*(3), 196.

5
Working with Risk

On reading this chapter you will:

- Understand the complexity of assessing and managing risk as a practitioner psychologist
- Be aware of the 'good practice' guidelines that are available and the suggested course of action when assessing risk
- Understand the importance of basing a risk assessment on a standardised approach
- Be aware of the role of the media in stigmatising individuals with mental illness as being prone to violent behaviour
- Understand what positive risk management is
- Understand the importance of working with the service user and establishing a trusting therapeutic relationship

Introduction

According to the Cambridge English Dictionary, risk is 'the possibility of something bad happening'. This is a general definition, where 'possibility' and 'bad' are subjective. That said, many have tried to capture what risk looks like so that safety is assured. In health and social care settings there are many risks, and practitioners should ensure they are informed of what these are and how to proceed. This chapter will examine how risk can be defined in health and social care, how a risk assessment is conducted, what is considered best practice, and how to manage risk. What will be reiterated more than once throughout this chapter is that eliminating risk is impossible. If we only look at our day-to-day lives and the risks we face (and potentially pose to others), we can see that our only protection is to make the most informed decision based on the information available to us. This is a particularly useful approach to more formal risk assessment and management.

Risk can present in many forms and it is an interesting reflective exercise to spend a few minutes thinking about what comes to mind as potential risk when working as a practitioner psychologist. A dominant theme might be the potential risk the service user poses to themselves or others as a result of significant mental health challenges – this is an area that tends to dominate the social discourse, particularly in the media. There are, however, far greater considerations. This chapter will look at the following principal themes from the perspective of the service user:

- Risk assessment
- Risk assessment tools
- Risk of violence
- Risk of self-harm or suicide
- Risk of self-neglect
- Safeguarding
- Risk management.

Matters of risk and mental health are a concern not only to health and social care services, but also to the general public. As noted by Lakeman (2006), concerns among the general public include perceptions of the danger posed by people with mental health problems, particularly the danger they pose to others. This has resulted in a focus on risk assessment as a quantifiable method of mitigating such risk. Risk assessment based on quantifiable factors will be considered later in the chapter, but ultimately it removes the saliency of clinical opinion. According to the UK Royal College of Psychiatrists (RCP, 2008), this results in overly coercive practice and policy which creates a culture of blame. It subsequently confirms the dominant view.

Competency in risk assessment and management is therefore a crucial skill for the practitioner psychologist. The aim is to take a more holistic perspective, acknowledging societal concerns and discourse, but also to push back against these forces and conduct clinically informed assessment and take informed action. From a professional skills perspective, competence in matters of risk is an ethical requirement, involves adopting an evidence based practice approach, requires practitioner self-awareness (reflective practice), supervision and leadership, and rests upon strong practitioner resilience. It is not an isolated endeavour. It involves shared perspectives across the service user, the family/carer, and other disciplines and agencies.

Risk Assessment

Information sharing and confidentiality

Before engaging in risk assessment and management, in most cases there may have been an event or situation that preceded a focus on risk. So that a coherent assessment is conducted, a full multidisciplinary response is required.

There needs to be agreement between agencies on how information is shared and which practices need to be put in place to mitigate issues related to different organisational systems (e.g. NHS systems versus those of the local authority). For example, computer systems or paper recording practices may differ, sometimes the terminology used may be qualitatively different, and there may be additional differences in thresholds for taking action. Ensuring the confidentiality of the information that is shared across agencies is also an important consideration, as is making sure the service user is fully informed about the limits to confidentiality. Where there are concerns about public protection, certain processes may need to be put in place, such as the Multi-Agency Public Protection Arrangement (MAPPA), which is an arrangement in England and Wales that was introduced by the Criminal Justice and Court Service Act 2000 (Department of Justice, 2000). The practitioner psychologist needs to familiarise themselves with such processes. Although such knowledge may be part of mandatory training in certain organisations, responsibility lies with the practitioner to gain this knowledge.

Collaborating with the service user and carer/family

When assessing risk, it is important that practitioner psychologists work with the service user and their carer/family to establish what to do when risk escalates, so that issues around breaking confidentiality and involving other agencies are clearly outlined. This gives the service user the opportunity to plan what this might look like in practice. It is about empowering the service user in the management of their care. The involvement of the service user and their carer means that any planned response is feasible, given the service user's situation.

It is important that the carer (or family) is supported to manage identified risks as they would typically be present at the time of risk escalation. Such support could involve providing information on key contacts or how to activate a pre-agreed action plan that has been put in place in collaboration with the service user. Although such planning will not mitigate the nature and severity of the risk in all cases, it will help the carer/family to cope with the situation that they are in, thus giving some support to their wellbeing as well as that of the service user (carers' needs should always be considered as part of a comprehensive assessment). Equally, if paid carers are involved, particularly if they change frequently, there should be a robust plan in place to fully inform them of the process to follow and indicators of risk. The caring role can be challenging, particularly when there are mental health problems and risk to self or others. For family members, the nature of this risk is even more profound. Ensure that you are aware of the support services that can help in a crisis situation so that you are able to provide the service user and their carers/family with this information.

Good practice in risk assessment

Assessing risk should be a part of day-to-day practice, and not an 'add on' when an individual service user presents as a risk. There needs to be a clear structure in place that is used regularly to make risk a consideration at each point of professional contact, such as noting a dip in mood, a change in routine, conflict. This should be embedded in team paperwork/practices so that there is a standard expectation and a standard response to factors that are notable in increasing risk.

It is not possible to eliminate risk, but it is possible to assess factors that indicate a higher likelihood of risk and to mitigate this likelihood with effective management. A great deal of research has focused on the construct of risk in order that assessments are evidence-based and therefore as accurate as can be. According to a briefing paper *Risk Assessment and Management* (Division of Clinical Psychology of the British Psychological Society, 2006), there are four main difficulties in applying evidence-based practice recommendations identified in research:

1. Conceptual difficulties, e.g. in defining what risk means.
2. Inconsistent and unclear outcomes used in validating risk assessment measures.
3. Lack of understanding about the relationship between risk indicators.
4. Risk assessment research often attempts to normalise a construct that, by its nature, presents differently across individuals.

The Royal College of Psychiatrists (RCP) published a good practice guide in 2016 on the assessment and management of risk to others (Royal College of Psychiatrists, 2016). It covers a number of elements that are relevant to practitioner psychologists and may mitigate some of the difficulties outlined above. In essence, it is the process of applying clinical expertise and service user values to the problematic 'best evidence' limitation. Although the original practice guidance specifically related to violence towards others, it is also relevant for all the kinds of risk discussed in this chapter. Good practice in risk assessment should therefore involve the following:

- Talking to the service user about their perspective on risk (what is their story?).
- Making sure you gain consent for a risk assessment and understanding what this might mean for the service user (the benefits and risks).
- Doing your homework: ensuring that you have all the information you need in order to conduct a comprehensive assessment (history taking and multidisciplinary information gathering).
- Avoiding taking things at face value (e.g. symptoms may indicate something other than the obvious).

- Considering how the condition might change over time and whether a repeat assessment should be conducted.
- Focusing on what you don't know rather than on what you do.
- Talking with your colleagues.
- Lead to making a formulation of risk (see below).

Of specific relevance is taking a full personal history, which may impact on the risk assessment, e.g. prior expressions of impulsiveness, recent stressors, things that have stopped risk escalation in the past. The environment is also an important consideration, for example whether the service user is in a restricted or unrestricted setting, the service user's access to materials that may increase the likelihood of risk escalation, the lack of support networks. As noted above, mental health can fluctuate and it is important to explore the service user's thinking during their narrative on risk and to consider 'invisible risk factors', such as lack of sleep, a high level of social media use or a lack of motivation (which are in stark contrast to more 'visible' risk factors, such as suicidal thoughts, heavy drinking or drug use, or specific threats). This sort of information can inform a risk formulation, which, according to the Royal College of Psychiatrists (2016), consists of (1) seriousness of risk, (2) immediacy of risk, (3) specificity of risk, (4) volatility of risk, (5) signs of increasing risk, and (6) what works in reducing the risk.

According to the Department of Health (2009), a risk formulation's intended purpose is to identify what may trigger the risk. They outline the more recognised psychological formulation of describing the predisposing, precipitating, perpetuating and protective factors. The Department of Health stipulate that there should be a plan attached to the formulation that should guide the team on what to do should there be warning signs of immediate risk. The plan should also note how the risk should be monitored, what therapeutic input is needed, and the impact on vocational activities, such as employment.

Conducting risk assessments should be done in a structured way to avoid missing important factors and to standardise the process (RCP, 2016). A structured approach will consider historical and current factors. Such an approach can be tailored to the specific service for which it is used, although it is also important not to make assumptions. For example, in a forensic setting, risk should not just be limited to criminal behaviour. A more standardised approach to clinical judgement is supported by the literature; for example, Woods (2013) highlighted the role of professional experience in clinical judgement. More experience may not necessarily mean a better assessment, and there will be differences in any assessment, but ensuring some structure in the process may mitigate these factors. What is clear, though, is that no piece of empirical research or individual clinical judgement can fully identify or even recognise all the relevant risk factors.

Actuarial systems and tools

A number of systems and tools have been developed in order that risk is evaluated based on empirical data, which may serve to support clinical judgement in a structured way. These systems and tools are termed 'actuarial' because they use statistical modelling to apply a form of measurement to risk assessment. Actuarial judgement uses statistical modelling to measure the *likelihood* of risk outcomes. Actuarial systems and tools look at the individual service user and measure the degree to which certain variables, such as age, gender, past criminal behaviour, predict risk outcomes (Division of Clinical Psychology, 2006). It should also be noted that some of these actuarial systems may only apply in certain settings or with certain risk factors.

A risk assessment tool should be one element of a thorough risk assessment as opposed to being a standalone assessment. Not all tools are created equal, so the practitioner must choose the correct tool (whether it is a standard tool for clinical judgement or an actuarial system). Table 5.1 provides an overview of some of these systems. The information has been drawn from the Division of Clinical Psychology's *Risk Assessment and Management* (2006) and the Department of Health's *Best Practice in Managing Risk* (2009).

Table 5.1   Examples of risk assessment tools

Structured clinical judgement tool: risk of violence, sexual violence, antisocial or offending behaviour	Brief description
HCR-20: Historical, Clinical, Risk management (Webster, Douglas, Eaves, & Hart, 1997)	A comprehensive tool consisting of 20 items that is broad in its application, with items that include clinical interviews, observation and clinical notes, focusing the current mental, emotional and behavioural presentation. This tool assesses the risk of violence. It is used by practitioner psychologists or related professionals, although training in its administration is advised.
PCL-R: Psychopathy Checklist-Revised (Harpur, Hare, & Hakstian, 1989)	An assessment tool consisting of a 20-item scale that is used as a measure of psychopathy traits and in diagnosing psychopathy. It is primarily used in forensic settings as a predictive tool for violence and antisocial and offending behaviour (although this is not advised by the test author). To administer this assessment, the practitioner needs a postgraduate qualification in a mental health profession and training.
Actuarial scales	
Static-2002R (Hanson, Lloyd, Helmus, & Thornton, 2012)	This is an actuarial tool that consists of 14 items which assesses the potential for sexual recidivism in adult male sex offenders. The items are based on fixed, historical events, e.g. prior sex offences. It has 5 main sub-scales: (1) age at release, (2) persistence of sexual offending, (3) sexual deviance, (4) relationship to victims, and (5) general criminality.

Table 5.1   (Continued)

Structured clinical judgement tool: risk of violence, sexual violence, antisocial or offending behaviour	Brief description
VRAG: Violence Risk Appraisal Guide (Quinsey, Harris, Rice, & Cormier, 2006).	This is an actuarial tool and consists of 12 items; one item uses the total score from the PCL-R tool (see above) and the remaining questions can be answered from the clinical file. No specific qualifications are needed to use this assessment tool.
Multiple risk	
RAMAS: Risk Assessment Management and Audit System (Hammond & O'Rourke, 2000)	A comprehensive tool that measures four types of risk: (1) dangerousness, (2) mental instability, (3) suicide/self-harm, and (4) vulnerability.
Risk of self-harm or suicide	
ASSIST: Applied Suicide Intervention Skills Training	Rather than being a measure or tool, ASSIST is a two-day, practice-based training programme designed for carers to help them care for individuals who have suicidal ideation/plans.
SADPERSONS (Patterson, Dohn, Bird, & Patterson, 1983)	This tool assesses the presence or absence of 10 risk factors. With the aid of cut-off scores, decisions can be made on whether there needs to be risk management. It is typically used as a screening tool in secondary mental health settings. Some of the cut-off score recommendations may not be relevant for a UK setting.
SIS: Suicidal Intent Scale (Beck, Schuyler, & Herman, 1974)	This scale can be used as an interview or as a self-administered scale. It is used for people who have attempted suicide and assesses their intention to die. There are 15 items that assess factors that relate to suicide attempt. A positive response to any of the scale items should be a cause for concern.

Risk assessment

In brief, the assessment of risk can be approached in three ways:

- Information obtained in an ongoing clinical assessment. This approach is regarded as inconsistent (Department of Health, 2009).
- The use of actuarial tools that assess static risk factors based on statistical modelling of risk potential.
- Structured clinical judgement can be achieved through a systematic and comprehensive assessment.

The structured clinical judgement approach is recommended by the Department of Health (2009) and the Royal College of Psychiatrists.

Risk of Violence

When conducting a search of the literature on assessing and managing the risk of violence, it is the literature on forensic settings that dominates. Of course, this is to be expected as it is logical to presume that those who pose a risk of violence to others, and are known to services, have a history of offending behaviour. Many of the assessment tools and scales discussed above target offending behaviour when considering risk (i.e. when violence is aimed at others). But violence can also target the self, as in self-harm and suicidal ideation, and can be a consequence of the symptoms of mental health problems or substance misuse (rather than an a premeditated intention to self-harm).

It is important to note that in common social discourse there is a belief, which has been fuelled culturally and through the media, where reports of violence by individuals with mental illness towards the public are sensationalised, that mental illness leads to dangerousness. As noted by Varshney, Mahapatra, Krishnan, Gupta and Deb (2016), there are only a small number of offenders who pose a risk of violence as a result of mental illness. Indeed, Varshney et al. emphasise the vulnerability of those with mental illness, who are often the victims of violence in the community. Taking into account factors such as young age, comorbid substance abuse problems and homelessness leading to a greater risk of victimisation, Varshney et al. ask the question: does victimisation predict violent behaviour or does violent behaviour predict victimisation, or both? From an assessment and management of risk perspective, the question illustrates the complexity and cross-over of multiple areas of risk, where the individual may be both a risk to others and at risk from others due to their vulnerability. When additional factors, such as substance abuse and severity of mental health problems, are key considerations and foci of intervention, the practitioner is faced with the task of holding multiple perspectives and requiring a wide range of competency in order to protect both the community and the individual.

Practitioner safety

An additional practice consideration is the risk of violence towards practitioners. There is a great deal of research in this area that discusses why this happens or how likely it is to happen, but the focus here will be on staying safe in practice. Despenser (2005) makes the salient point that practitioner safety tends to be a neglected topic. Despenser's central message is that practitioner safety is equally as important as service user safety, and that assessment of practitioner safety is essential. The following factors should be considered (this is not an exhaustive list and the nature of the setting and organisation is also a key consideration):

- Alarm systems and safety protocols for practitioners who work in isolation or in private practice.
- The layout of the therapy space so that the practitioner is closer to the exit.
- Furnishings in the room in case they may become a source of risk.
- Service user's history/source of referral – are there any known or unknown risk factors?
- Listening to your 'gut reaction' and discussing any worries in supervision.
- The opportunity to 'debrief' with someone after sessions.
- The nature of any potential violence, whether it may be psychological or physical.

Of course, the practitioner can refuse to work with a service user if any of these factors makes them feel uneasy. Although the likelihood of harm befalling a practitioner is small, it is nonetheless valid. It is important to note that even if a practitioner works in a setting where service users have a past history of violence and there is an expectation that practitioners are working with risk daily, such as in a forensic setting, it is still vital that the practitioner removes themselves from any situation that creates discomfort. Focused reflection and discussion with peers may unearth why such feelings of discomfort occurred, but careful consideration of such issues should be given in all health and social care settings.

Violence against the Self

The Royal College of Psychiatrists' report *Self-harm, Suicide and Risk: Helping People who Self-harm* (2010: 6) defines 'self-harm' as 'an intentional act of self-poisoning or self-injury irrespective of the type of motivation or degree of suicidal intent'. This quote illustrates differences in motivation; the act of self-harm may indicate a wish to die or it may be a way to relieve distressing emotions or distract from intolerable situations. There are multiple motivations for self-harming behaviour (Loughry & Kerr, 1989). The Royal College of Psychiatrists (2010) notes that risk assessments related to self-harm and suicidal intent are limited in their predictive utility, so the nature of risk assessment in this domain is challenging.

The National Institute for Health and Care Excellence (NICE, 2011) has published clinical guidelines for the long-term management of self-harm, which includes a list of key priorities for implementation. The clinical guidelines recommend that risk assessment tools and scales are not used to predict future suicide or the repetition of self-harming behaviours. It is important to unpick this somewhat, given that there are validated assessment tools that practitioners can use (e.g. the Suicidal Intent Scale; Beck et al., 1974), and the reader may be questioning this contradiction. A risk assessment has a number of functions when considering any factor, but for self-harm and suicidal intent this includes:

- Informing an intervention (including therapeutic/placement/care provision).
- Categorising a service user as 'high' versus 'low' risk as a guide for service provision.
- Establishing risk to life (now or in the future).

Assessment tools and scales may indicate the nature of the current behaviour, intent and risk, but they cannot determine future risk or specify a 'category' of risk. To put this in context, a current incidence of self-harm or an attempted suicide can be considered 'low risk', depending on the circumstances of the event, but this should not be used to categorise a service user as at future 'low risk' (in so doing, excluding that service user from service input and intervention).

As noted by Large, Ryan, Carter and Kapur (2017), there is little evidence to suggest that self-harm and suicide assessment tools and scales are useful in decision making. Large and colleagues emphasise that all individuals presenting to services following episodes of self-harm or when voicing suicidal intent should be offered evidence-based interventions following an assessment of the event and identification of treatable factors. They suggest that rather than using an assessment to categorise an individual into a 'high'- or 'low'-risk group, the primary objective should be to establish what the person needs. In approaching an individual who may be suicidal, the emphasis should be on listening to what the person says, staying respectful, understanding the person's story and not assuming that non-expression of suicidal ideation means that there is none.

Assessing risk of self-harm

NICE (2011) guidelines state that assessing risk of self-harm should include consideration of the following:

- The nature of current and past self-harming behaviours.
- The nature of current and past suicidal intent.
- Symptoms of depression or the presence of psychiatric illness and its relationship to the self-harming behaviours.
- The personal and social context of triggers for self-harming behaviours.
- The nature and function of social, psychological, pharmacological and motivational triggers or protective factors associated with self-harming behaviours.
- Coping strategies (to reduce or remove self-harming behaviour and to contain the impact of self-harming behaviour).
- Relationships that are supportive or that might trigger self-harming behaviour.
- Immediate risks and long-term risks of self-harming behaviours.

Practice considerations

Health Education England (HEE) has produced comprehensive competence frameworks for self-harm and suicide prevention for children and young people and adults and older adults (Health Education England, 2018), and these can be a helpful starting point for the reader. For the purposes of this chapter, the focus will be on adults and older adults. The framework recommends the skills and knowledge that practitioners need in order to assess risk of self-harm and suicide. According to the framework, some of the primary considerations are the following:

- Collaborating with the service user – developing trust and empowering the individual to make choices. This includes encouraging support networks such as families, carers and their wider social network, including significant others.
- Sharing information – maintaining confidentiality can become a challenging issue for practitioners with a duty to protect.
- Managing transitions in service delivery – changes in service provision can occur for a variety of reasons, including moving from one service to another due to age (e.g. CAMHS to Adult services). Transitions mean that existing trusted relationships will need to end and that new relationships will need to develop, and can be a cause of stressors that can exacerbate the presenting risk issue.

Interacting with people who have self-harmed or who express suicidal ideation

Best practice when people self-harm or express suicidal ideation is to show empathy and to recognise that the individual's perspective and concerns are valid and deserving of compassion. It is possible that initial responses to the individual's distress may have involved negative emotions or responses from those closest to the individual, and therefore it is imperative that responses from practitioners do not alienate the individual further.

Self-neglect

Over and above the focus on dangerousness and self-harm, an important area that is often overlooked in our interactions with service users is the risk of service user self-neglect. A comprehensive definition of self-neglect covers three main areas: (1) physical or mental illness as a result of neglect, (2) relapse of mental illness, causing physical harm through self-neglect or non-adherence to treatment, and (3) the presence of environmental health problems that pose a risk to the individual or others they interact with (Morgan, 1998).

In a qualitative study of how mental health workers assess and manage the risk of self-neglect, Gunstone (2003) highlights how this is a 'grey area' in clinical practice. Gunstone recommends that self-neglect is given the same focus and consideration as dangerousness and self-harm and suicidal ideation. What is notable in this particular study is the reluctance of practitioners to employ specific assessment tools when working with self-neglect. They stated that the available tools are not individualised to the service user and are primarily used for research. Regarding clinical assessment, then, decision-making should be based on obtaining a full clinical history and conducting an assessment that focuses on the individual's needs and wishes.

Interventions in cases of self-neglect

Whether or not to intervene in cases of self-neglect should be based on the following (Gunstone, 2003):

- A mental health capacity assessment.
- If capacity is established, is there imminent risk of harm to the service user from self-neglect?
- If there is an imminent risk of harm, work with the service user to minimise the impact of the most immediate issue.
- If there is not an imminent risk, work with the service user to develop a long-term management plan (that includes intervention if necessary).
- Balance the views of others with those of the individual, that is, what others deem to be unacceptable self-neglect needs to be balanced with the autonomy of the individual in determining what is unacceptable to them.
- Consider the environmental impact (e.g. hoarding behaviours) in relation to local authority regulations and the law.

Safeguarding

According to the BPS's *Practice Guidelines*, the definition of an adult at risk of harm is as follows:

> An adult at risk of harm is a person aged 18 or over with need for care or support, who is experiencing, or is at risk of, abuse or neglect, and as a result of their needs is unable to protect himself or herself against the abuse or neglect or the risk of it. The needs referred to here may cover a variety of personal or life circumstances including (but not limited to) cognitive impairment, age, disability, illness, injury or mental health condition. (British Psychological Society, 2017: 41)

There is no one piece of legislation that exists for safeguarding adults at risk of harm, but the Care Act 2014 (Department of Health, 2014) can be used as a framework for practice. Adults at risk of harm can be found across all sections of society, regardless of gender, age, ability, sexual orientation, religion, race, ethnicity or socio-economic circumstances. In identifying what constitutes abuse, the BPS's *Practice Guidelines* offers a comprehensive list which is based in legislation and are not stand-alone categories (i.e. abuse may span more than one category):

- Physical abuse
- Sexual violence and abuse
- Emotional abuse
- Financial abuse
- Institutional abuse
- Neglect (BPS, 2017).

Adult safeguarding boards

Adult safeguarding boards are based within localities to ensure that safeguarding arrangements are in place, as laid out by the Care Act 2014. It is the responsibility of the local authority to set up adult safeguarding boards. Safeguarding adults involves protecting them from abuse and neglect, so they may live safely. Collaborative working among organisations to stop this happening and to remove the risk of this happening, the active promotion of wellbeing and recognising that some adults may not have awareness of risks to their safety and wellbeing.

The safeguarding principles of adult safeguarding boards

There are six safeguarding principles outlined by the Care Act 2014, which underpin the work of adult safeguarding boards:

1. Empowerment: people are supported and encouraged to make their own decisions and to give informed consent.
2. Prevention: it is better to take action before harm occurs.
3. Proportionality: the least intrusive response appropriate to the risk presented is followed.
4. Protection: support for and representation of those in greatest need.
5. Partnership: local solutions through services working with their communities – communities have a part to play in preventing, detecting and reporting neglect and abuse.
6. Accountability and transparency in safeguarding practice.

Safeguarding is the responsibility of everyone, across private and public organisations, whether in hospitals, care homes, general practice or community care. Each organisation will have its own safeguarding policy. It is your responsibility as a practitioner psychologist to familiarise yourself with local processes for assessment and referral to the appropriate team. Safeguarding should be a core concern when assessing risk in general, particularly where certain risk behaviours impact on others, such as carers, family members and the wider support network.

Risk Management

There is a range of guidance documents that can be used by the practitioner in determining levels of risk and establishing an effective management plan. In a similar manner to ethical codes of practice and values, approaches to risk management are often based on sets of principles. The Department of Health document *Best Practice in Managing Risk* (2009) emphasises the following principles:

- Positive risk management
- Adopting a collaborative approach with the service user and their carers/ family
- Focusing on the service user's strengths
- Determining organisational versus individual practitioner roles in risk management.

These principles recommend the need for a measured and informed approach. They are also supported by the Royal College of Psychiatrist's good practice guide '*Assessment and Management of Risk to Others*', which can be found in the Royal College of Psychiatrists college report (CR201) 'Rethinking Risk to Others in Mental Health Services' (2016) that adds the principles of being ready 'to take action', 'to reduce distress', and 'to act with empathy and compassion'.

In terms of what works in reducing risk, there needs to be a focus on safety (towards the self and others). Capacity needs to be considered as well as the service user's willingness to engage. These factors are recorded in the service user's notes and should be subject to regular review. There may need to be provision for support in an in-patient setting, should risk factors prevent the service user remaining in the community. Other services within the community that serve a key role in managing risk are social service support, forensic and offender teams, substance misuse services and safeguarding teams.

The management of risk can be guided by the Mental Health Act 1983 (Department of Health, 1983) when detainment is necessary due to risk factors arising from mental health difficulties. If medication is needed, engaging the service user in taking that medication is a vital part of risk management. In home settings, it may be difficult to manage. Decisions must also be made about who is clinically responsible for care provision and care planning. Information regarding the treatment and management plan needs to be comprehensive.

Positive risk management

Rather than attempts to eliminate all risks, which may be punitive and restrictive for the service user, positive risk management aims to give service users some choice and control in their lives. It requires collaboration with and consideration of the service user's quality of life and aims to balance what makes their life meaningful with their own safety and the safety of others. Research by Szmukler and Rose (2013) discusses the relevance of trust when considering the balance between adopting positive risk management processes and more defensive strategies. According to Szmukler and Rose, the service user needs to be able to trust that the practitioner has no hidden agenda, something that can be particularly challenging for individuals who, by the nature of their mental health condition, are acutely uncertain of their own judgement of others. What is key is effective communication.

Unfortunately, adopting formal risk assessment procedures at an early stage in the practitioner and service user relationship, with paperwork being the dominant form of record, emphasises that organisational needs and the needs of others hold greater importance than the needs of the service user. When considering the principles put forward by the Department of Health (2009), the practitioner may be faced with competing organisational demands (e.g. completing formalised risk assessments) and service user needs (e.g. within the therapeutic relationship). Practitioner competence is key in being able to hold both demands: to evidence and formally record the risk assessment and management plan as well as collaborating effectively with the service user.

Summary

This chapter has provided an overview of what risk is, and how it is defined and managed in practice. The nature of risk and its assessment, and the range of approaches to do this, have been discussed, with standardised, structured clinical judgement being the preferred approach. A key aspect is the importance of collaborating with the service user, their family/carer and other agencies.

Although the assessment of risk is the primary objective, providing or arranging sources of support for the family/carer is also good practice. The family/carer is typically the first in line when there is a potential for risk escalation, and they are key in contributing to the risk assessment and in risk management plans.

There are challenges in conducting a risk assessment based on research evidence alone – as a construct, risk is subject to conceptual difficulties in the literature. Good practice in risk assessment involves clinical judgement and value-based systems. Risk of violence to others is the area that we would consider to be most in need of risk assessment and management, but we also need to consider risk to self, in the form of self-harm, suicidal ideation or self-neglect.

Knowledge of what safeguarding is in health and social care and how this works in practice is also a key area. Practitioner safety is an often-neglected but essential consideration. When considering risk management, a balance needs to be struck between safety and positive risk management approaches which rely on less restrictive and punitive measures.

Key Points

- Risk is something that is driven by social discourse and the media.
- Practitioner psychologists should be knowledgable on how to assess and manage risk and to do so in collaboration with the service user.
- It is not only about assessing risk, but also about creating a formulation and providing an intervention.
- Best practice suggests that risk assessment should involve a structured clinical judgement.
- Positive risk management invovles balancing service user needs and values and their safety and the safety of others.

Practice Case Studies

Case Study 1

You are a Forensic Psychologist working in a medium secure unit and your day-to-day work involves carrying out one-to-one assessments of offenders with a focus on risk assessment and risk management. The aim of your service is to rehabilitate offenders who have a diagnosed mental illness. You have met with a new inmate, David, who has been placed on a hospital order (section 37, which is a minimum six-month stay followed by release into the community) following a conviction for assault and robbery. David has a diagnosis of bipolar disorder.

You have only met David once and he has told you that his mental health contributed to his offending behaviour and that his guilt over what he'd done is now weighing heavily on him. He feels unsafe and that he may harm himself. He presents as low in mood and dishevelled. According to the prison guard, David has not been eating or had any visitors.

David was happy to provide a limited amount of information but was silent for much of the interview. You have asked David if you can speak with his family and he has agreed. You also have access to a range of community support agencies in the area where David lives.

Suggested questions

1. What are the *potential* risk issues that should be considered in this case?
2. What professional skills (outlined in this book) would be most helpful/appropriate?

Case Study 2

You are a Counselling Psychologist working in an adult mental health team. You have a new referral to meet Gill, who is her mid-30s and has a history of anxiety and depression. You ring the referring GP to ask if there were any updates (the referral had been waiting for six months) and they inform you that Gill had to be removed from the surgery a few weeks ago due to threats made against the receptionist. There was no apparent cause other than an extensive waiting time due to an emergency situation.

The GP provides further background: Gill lives alone and is isolated from her family. She works part time. She is not on any medication for anxiety or depression. As far as you are aware, Gill hasn't been seen by any other mental health practitioner. You attend clinical supervision and discuss your concerns about working with Gill. As you have not met her yet, you have little objective information to reflect upon and your clinical supervisor assures you that meeting Gill in a busy office environment will ensure that should anything happen, you will be safe. You feel embarrassed that it had worried you so much.

You arrange a first session with Gill and make sure that you choose a room that is close to reception, and that you sit by the door. There is also a phone in the room, so you are able to phone a colleague for 'advice' should the need arise (this is an established in-service safety mechanism for staff when working alone with service users).

Your first session with Gill is fine. There are no indicators of any threat or emotional dysregulation or behaviour that could be a cause for concern. Gill even refers to the GP situation and says it was a moment of poor judgement and she is mortified that she behaved in that way. Despite this, you can't help but feel unsure of Gill and you have a gut feeling that your first impressions are not necessarily accurate. You are also telling yourself that you are just being overly cautious and that there is nothing to worry about. Your next session with Gill is scheduled for a week's time.

Suggested questions

1. Would this situation necessitate a formal risk assessment? Explain your rationale.
2. How might you approach this situation during your next clinical supervision?

References

Beck, A. T., Schuyler, D., & Herman, I. (1974). *Development of Suicidal Intent Scales*. Philadelphia, PA: Charles Press Publishers.

British Psychological Society. (2017) *Practice Guidelines*. Leicester: BPS. Retrieved from www.bps.org.uk/sites/www.bps.org.uk/files/Policy/Policy%20-%20Files/BPS%20Practice%20Guidelines%20%28Third%20Edition%29.pdf

Department of Health. (1983). *Mental Health Act (1983)*. London: HMSO. Available at www.legislation.gov.uk/ukpga/1983/20/contents (accessed: 2 February 2021).

Department of Health. (2009). *Best Practice in Managing Risk: Principles and Evidence for Best Practice in the Assessment and Management of Risk to Self and Others in Mental Health Services*. London: HMSO.

Department of Health. (2014). *Care Act (2014)*. London: HMSO. Available at www.legislation.gov.uk/ukpga/2014/23/contents/enacted (accessed: 2 February 2021).

Department of Justice. (2000). *Criminal Justice and Court Services Act (2000)*. London: HMSO. Available at www.legislation.gov.uk/ukpga/2000/43/contents (accessed: 2 February 2021).

Despenser, S. (2005). The personal safety of the therapist. *Psychodynamic Practice*, *11*(4), 429–446.

Division of Clinical Psychology of the British Psychological Society. (2006). *Risk Assessment and Management*. Leicester: British Psychological Society.

Gunstone, S. (2003). Risk assessment and management of patients with self-neglect: A 'grey area' for mental health workers. *Journal of Psychiatric and Mental Health Nursing, 10*(3), 287–296.

Hammond S., & O'Rourke M. (2000) *A Psychometric Model of Risk Assessment*. London: Department of Health.

Hanson, R. K., Lloyd, C. D., Helmus, L., & Thornton, D. (2012). Developing non-arbitrary metrics for risk communication: Percentile ranks for the Static-99/R and Static-2002/R sexual offender risk tools. *International Journal of Forensic Mental Health, 11*(1), 9–23.

Harpur, T. J., Hare, R. D., & Hakstian, A. R. (1989). Two-factor conceptualization of psychopathy: Construct validity and assessment implications. *Psychological Assessment: A Journal of Consulting and Clinical Psychology, 1*(1), 6.

Health Education England. (2018). *Self-harm and suicide prevention competence framework*. Available at www.ucl.ac.uk/pals/sites/pals/files/self-harm_and_suicide_prevention_competence_framework_-_adults_and_older_adults_8th_oct_18.pdf (accessed: 2 February 2021).

Lakeman, R. (2006). An anxious profession in an age of fear. *Journal of Psychiatric and Mental Health Nursing, 13*(4), 395–400.

Large, M. M., Ryan, C. J., Carter, G., & Kapur, N. (2017). Can we usefully stratify patients according to suicide risk? *BMJ, 359*. https://doi.org/10.1136/bmj.j4627

Loughrey, G., & Kerr, A. (1989). Motivation in deliberate self-harm. *The Ulster Medical Journal, 58*(1), 46.

Morgan, S. (1998). The assessment and management of risk. In C. Brooker & J. Repper (Eds.), *Serious Mental Health Problems in the Community: Policy, Practice and Research* (pp. 263–290). London: Bailliere Tindall.

NICE (National Institute for Health and Care Excellence). (2011). *Self-harm in Over 8s: Long-term Management* [NICE Guideline No. 133]. London: NICE. www.nice.org.uk/guidance/cg133

Patterson, W. M., Dohn, H. H., Bird, J., & Patterson, G. A. (1983). Evaluation of suicidal patients: The SAD PERSONS scale. *Psychosomatics, 24*(4), 343–349.

Quinsey, V. L., Harris, G. T., Rice, M. E., & Cormier, C. A. (2006). *Violent Offenders: Appraising and Managing Risk.* Washington, DC: American Psychological Association.

Royal College of Psychiatrists. (2010). *Self-harm, Suicide and Risk: Helping People who Self-harm* (Council Report 158). London: Royal College of Psychiatrists.

Royal College of Psychiatrists. (2016). *Rethinking Risk to Others in Mental Health Services* (Council Report 201). London: Royal College of Psychiatrists.

Szmukler, G., & Rose, N. (2013). Risk assessment in mental health care: Values and costs. *Behavioral Sciences & the Law, 31*(1), 125–140.

Varshney, M., Mahapatra, A., Krishnan, V., Gupta, R., & Deb, K. S. (2016). Violence and mental illness: What is the true story? *Journal of Epidemiology and Community Health, 70*(3), 223–225.

Webster, C. D., Douglas, K. S., Eaves, D., & Hart, S. D. (1997). *HCR-20: Assessing the Risk of Violence. Version 2.* Burnaby, BC: Simon Fraser University and Forensic Psychiatric Services Commission of British Columbia.

Woods, P. (2013). Risk assessment and management approaches on mental health units. *Journal of Psychiatric and Mental Health Nursing, 20*(9), 807–813.

6

Equality and Diversity

On reading this chapter you will:

- Understand the function of the Equality Act 2010
- Understand the regulatory and legal aspects of equality
- Understand the skills and competencies required for anti-discriminatory practice
- Appreciate the impact of discrimination on service users
- Be able to critically explore your own understanding of discrimination and reflect on what this means for you as a practitioner psychologist
- Understand the importance of challenging discrimination within the workplace and within your profession

Introduction

This chapter will first consider the legal impact of the Equality Act 2010 (Government Equalities Office, 2010), which aims to protect people against discrimination in employment and as consumers of public and private services. The chapter will then outline the professional climate and the skills and actions that the practitioner psychologist will rely on not only to keep within the law, but also to uphold the professional body requirements. Suggestions are made as to how to identify discrimination and the actions needed to challenge such discrimination. As such, it will form a 'good practice guide' for the practitioner psychologist. For more in-depth legal and technical information, readers should consult *The Equality Act 2010 in Mental Health: A Guide to Implementation and Issues for Practice*, edited by Sewell (2012), which is an accessible and informative text on the subject.

The Legal Perspective

The Equality Act 2010

The Equality Act 2010 brings together a range of primary and secondary legislation (including the Disability Discrimination Act 1995, the Race Relations
Act 1976, the Sex Discrimination Act 1975) and is the largest piece of anti-
discrimination legislation that the UK has known. It covers England, Wales and
Scotland, and some sections apply to Northern Ireland. This is civil law and is
primarily enforced by individuals. It aims to protect people against discrimination, harassment or victimisation in the workplace and protects users of public
or private services. These aims relate to a series of 'protected characteristics'.

Protected Characteristics in the Equality Act 2010

- *Age* – this includes a specific age or an age range.
- *Disability* – physical or mental impairment which has a substantial and long-term
  adverse effect on being able to carry out normal day-to-day activities.
- *Gender reassignment* – a person is proposing to undergo, is undergoing or has
  undergone a process of reassigning the person's sex by changing physiological or
  other attributes of sex; a reference to a transexual person is reference to the
  protected characteristic of gender reassignment.
- *Marriage and civil partnership* – to be married or be part of a civil partnership.
- *Pregnancy and maternity*.
- *Race* – this includes skin colour, nationality, ethnic or national origins.
- *Religion or belief* – this includes a lack of religion or belief; the term 'belief' includes
  religious or philosophical belief.
- *Sex* – reference to a man or a woman or persons of the same sex.
- *Sexual orientation* – this includes sexual orientation towards (1) persons of the
  same sex, (2) persons of the opposite sex, or (3) persons of either sex.

The Act also lists different types of discrimination.

Direct discrimination

Direct discrimination occurs where a person is treated less favourably than
others because of a protected characteristic. There are caveats, such as age,
where age may limit the achievement of a legitimate aim. Direct discrimination

may also occur as a result of two or more protected characteristics. Disability discrimination occurs if a person is treated unfavourably as a result of that person's disability and this treatment is not proportionate to the achievement of a legitimate aim.

Indirect discrimination

Indirect discrimination occurs where a person is discriminated against as a result of a 'provision, criterion or practice' that discriminates against a relevant protected characteristic. Here, the provision, criterion or practice has the effect of excluding that individual as a result of the protected characteristic in comparison to other people to whom it applies. An example of indirect discrimination might be an age requirement where age is not relevant to the duties of the role.

Other conduct that is prohibited by the Act is harassment and victimisation. Harassment is where a person engages in unwanted conduct towards another person by virtue of a protected characteristic, with the purpose of violating their dignity, and in creating an intimidating environment. This includes conduct of a sexual nature. Victimisation is where a person subjects another person to detriment as a result of that person engaging in a protected act, or a belief that the person has engaged in a protected act. This is where a person is singled out because they have made a complaint or challenged others in relation to the Equality Act 2010.

Of particular relevance is the duty to make reasonable adjustments for a disabled person. According to the Equality Act 2010, there is a duty to make reasonable adjustments and these are underpinned by three requirements:

1. If a provision, criterion or practice puts a disabled person at substantial disadvantage in comparison to others, the person on whom the duty is imposed must take reasonable steps to avoid the disadvantage.
2. That the person on whom the duty is imposed avoids substantial disadvantage as a result of a physical feature (such as providing a ramp/lift suitable for wheelchair access where there would otherwise only be stairs).
3. That the person on whom the duty is imposed provides a piece of equipment or technology without which, the disabled person is put at substantial disadvantage in comparison to non-disabled people.

It is further stipulated that the disabled person should not have to pay for such adjustments. The information contained in the Act relating to types of discrimination and the duty therein is far more exhaustive than what can be described here, and readers would be advised to explore the Act directly for more information.

The Equality Act 2010 states that public bodies or those carrying out public functions, such as the NHS, must comply with the public sector equality duty. The equality duty ensures that a public body, such as the NHS, considers the needs of all individuals, including their employees, in shaping policy and in delivering services. The equality duty has three aims:

1. To remove unlawful discrimination – this includes harassment and victimi-sation as well as other conduct prohibited by the Act.
2. To maintain equality of opportunity – between people who share the pro-tected characteristics and those who don't.
3. To ensure good relations – between people who share a protected char-acteristic and people who don't.

There has to be conscious thought given to these three aims by public bodies and it may involve making provision for what may be wanted by those without the protected characteristics (e.g. car parking provision for those who are una-ble to use public transport but otherwise have no protected characteristics).

Breaching the Equality Act 2010

Should someone be discriminated against, harassed or victimised, an individual claim can be made to the county court. These claims normally have to be made by the person against whom the discrimination has occurred, within six months of the incident, but this can sometimes be extended by the court. Such a course of action can be expensive and time-consuming, not to mention a highly stress-ful experience. It is possible that the claimant may have to pay the legal costs of the other party should they lose the case in court. The person or organisation that the claim is being made against (the defendant) must be informed that the person wants to take action. This is known as the 'letter before claim', and gives the defendant an opportunity to write back and explain their position, and to see whether a solution can be found to avoid court action. The test for proving discrimination is to demonstrate that a person has been treated less favourably than another person because of a reason related to a protected characteristic (the comparator test); it should be noted that the test is not that someone has been treated unfairly against an absolute standard.

The Good Practice Perspective

The Equality Act 2010 provides specific duties for public bodies and public services but does not provide the practitioner psychologist with clear practice guidelines. Practitioner psychologists can never be completely objective and free of bias. While acknowledging that this can lead to ethical dilemmas (Shiles, 2009), the practitioner is still expected to manage this lack of objectivity so that best practice is maintained. Because practitioners have a range of backgrounds and values, it is impossible to create a 'one size fits all' set of guidelines that practitioners can follow when they are faced with ethical dilemmas related to equality and diversity. In addition, diversity is a concept that has no fixed meaning and can be construed to meet others' social motivations (Unzueta, Knowles, & Ho, 2012). Nevertheless, despite the lack of concrete guidelines, the practitioner can consult the Health and Care Professions Council's (HCPC) (2016) standards of conduct, performance and ethics, which state that registrants must challenge discrimination as follows:

- By not discriminating against service users, carers or colleagues and allowing this to affect professional relationships and treatment provision.
- By challenging colleagues whom the practitioner believes have discriminated against service users, carers and colleagues.

Organisations will also have policies and structures in place, as well as mandatory training (more of this later), which is generally for all personnel so will not be specific to a particular profession. Clinical supervision, and in particular engaging in reflective practice, will help the practitioner to identify areas of concern or areas for development (or good practice!). This should incorporate not only personal biases and prejudices, but also the experience of being discriminated against. Challenging discrimination is a particularly difficult area, and having a strong commitment to identifying values and leadership practices that can help the practitioner to deal with such professional dilemmas is key.

A Model of Anti-discriminatory Practice for Practitioner Psychologists

In writing this chapter, it became clear that there are many facets to discrimination and it can be difficult to give due consideration to each of those facets, in enough depth, to truly capture its importance in the work of a psychologist. So that such consideration is given to the breadth of equality and diversity skills and knowledge in psychology practice, Figure 6.1 shows the three arms of anti-discriminatory practice as an outline of topics discussed in this chapter.

Interpersonal Discrimination

When asked about discrimination, it is often the case that the practitioner psychologist will immediately think about their therapeutic practice and relationships with service users. However, discrimination can come from the service user towards the practitioner (who may belong to one or more minority groups), or between the practitioner and colleagues or peers, or between the

Figure 6.1   The three arms of anti-discriminatory practice

service user and their family or carers. Discrimination from outside the therapy room is just as important as it will influence the therapeutic relationship and should therefore be subject to reflection.

Micro-aggressions

Discriminatory practices related to the protected characteristics may appear obvious and easy to identify, but in practice this may not be the case. Despite living in a society that purports to welcome diversity, discrimination towards all people is often evident in subtle prejudice, which is often described as 'micro-aggressions'. Sue (2010: 24) defines micro-aggressions as 'the everyday verbal, nonverbal, and environmental slights, snubs, or insults, whether intentional or unintentional, which communicate hostile, derogatory, or negative messages to target persons based solely upon their marginalized group membership'. Micro-aggressions affect everyone (e.g. in relation to race, sex and gender), yet because they are subtle, such behaviour is hard to recognise and, sadly, for some, may not be taken as seriously as a more obvious transgression. As noted by Sue and colleagues (2007), it is often the case that the perpetrator will believe that the person who is subject to the micro-aggression is overreacting, and that most incidents are seen as trivial. A further complication is that the reaction to the micro-aggression is based on factors such as recognising it as a micro-aggression in the first place, not knowing how to respond, rationalising the behaviour (e.g. 'they didn't mean it', 'nothing will come of it anyway', etc.), denying the behaviour (e.g. 'I imagined it'), and fearing negative consequences towards the recipient (Sue et al., 2007).

The study of micro-aggressions targeting race, ethnicity and sexual orientation in therapy demonstrates that service users do perceive micro-aggressions in therapy (Shelton & Delgado-Romero, 2013; Owen, Tao, Imel, Wampold, & Rodolfa, 2014). According to Owen and colleagues (2014), they impact on the therapeutic alliance regardless of the mental health status of the service user or the therapist's racial and ethnic identity. An example of a micro-aggression against sexual orientation might be a therapist asking a married male service user 'What is your wife's name?', presuming a heterosexual orientation (Shelton & Delgado-Romero, 2013).

Peters, Schwenk, Ahlstrom and McIalwain (2017) focused on how people with mental illness experienced micro-aggressions. Qualitative data was gathered to investigate the types of micro-aggression that were experienced, and the following themes were identified:

- Conveying stereotypes about individuals with mental illness – assumptions based on stereotypes were often experienced by participants, e.g. inferiority, weakness, attention-seeking, etc.
- Invalidating the experience of having a mental illness – participants experienced others' doubt of the existence of the condition, the severity of the condition, and avoiding explicit acknowledgement of the condition.
- Defining a person by their disorder – participants reported that they were ignored and people focused on the mental illness instead.
- Misusing terminology – terminology relating to mental illness being used incorrectly, e.g. people can often say things such as 'I'm so OCD because…' when they are not actually suffering from obsessive-compulsive disorder.

Although other minority groups may experience different forms of micro-aggressions, practitioners need to understand the impact of micro-aggressions so that such events or assumptions can be recognised and acknowledged.

Peters and colleagues (2017) found that perpetrators of micro-aggressions were identified as professionals, family and friends. A further complication in identifying a micro-aggression is that, in comparison to more obvious and identifiable discrimination, the person on the receiving end of the micro-aggression is often left feeling confused and questioning whether the experience is actually an offence (Sue, 2010). Given the Equality Act 2010 (Government Equalities Office, 2010), how useful is this legal stance in the face of such ambiguity? The impact of micro-aggression is undeniable, and is often neglected when formulating a service user's presentation.

Discrimination against the practitioner psychologist

The literature is sparse when it is the practitioner who is on the receiving end of discrimination, whether overtly or in the form of micro-aggressions. There is no consideration of this area of practice in the HCPC's *Standards of Conduct, Performance and Ethics* (2016) or in the British Psychological Society's *Practice Guidelines* (2017b). Other than supervision as a forum to discuss such experiences, how should the practitioner negotiate such occurrences in the therapy room? The following is a set of ideas that have been garnered from informal discussion with colleagues, and are suggestions based on others' experiences:

- It is important for the practitioner to be aware of their own areas of discomfort relating to diversity and culture, and to be able to hold an open discussion with service users, if appropriate, to place potential perceived discrimination in context. For example, a service user's hostility might be misinterpreted as discriminatory when it could more likely be a consequence of the service user's situation. It might represent a topic on which to base an open discussion about biases in therapy. Of course, 'calling out' a perceived discriminatory response by the service user may do more harm than good, and it may be better to explore the issue within the therapeutic relationship. For example, in the case of a potential gender or race issue, you might introduce the topic as: 'You seem to be uneasy talking about your situation with me; why don't we spend a few minutes talking about what this feels like for you?' This approach opens the door to discussing potential bias and prejudice should they be present.
- Although I have stated that 'calling out' a discriminatory comment may not be the best idea, it is sometimes good to be direct. For some practitioners, should persistent micro-aggressions towards them occur, calling out such behaviour could be done in a way that accepts the service user for who they are, while honestly stating the experience from the practitioner's point of view. For example, if a service user keeps making reference to a practitioner's age, they could say: 'How do you feel about working with a therapist who is younger than you? Is this something that makes you feel uncomfortable?'
- When the service user makes obvious derogatory remarks or there are instances when the practitioner feels uncomfortable with what is being said or implied behaviourally, then it may be necessary to re-establish boundaries, i.e. that such behaviour will not be tolerated and that the session

will have to come to an end if the behaviour persists. There should be protocols in place for this very situation, and if there are none, then they should be established. Such encounters may lead to a break in the therapeutic relationship, and the service user may need to be re-allocated to another colleague if the practitioner no longer wishes to work with them. Of course, this should be dealt with in supervision and in collaboration with senior leadership. A question that should be asked within a service is 'What constitutes behaviour that means a service user should be excluded from accessing that particular service?'.

• Make sure you look after your own wellbeing and seek support from supervisors and colleagues. Transgressions can lead to negative emotions, which, if repeated over time, can have an accumulative effect. All instances of discrimination are painful. Sharing these experiences also allows learning and development among colleagues, and creates a safe and supportive environment.

Challenging assumptions

Schmitt, Branscombe, Postmes and Garcia (2014), in a comprehensive meta-analysis of research exploring the impact of discrimination across a range of minority groups, found that pervasive discrimination resulted in a greater impact upon wellbeing than did isolated events. There is nothing more pervasive and damaging than unchallenged assumptions that persist unless explicitly identified and questioned. The following set of questions may guide the practitioner psychologist in reflecting upon the assumptions that are made (or that they make). They can also be used as a focus in training or supervision.

1. What assumptions do I make about people?
2. Why do I come to the conclusions that I do?
3. When do these assumptions occur?
4. How can these assumptions cause difficulty?
5. How can I challenge these assumptions effectively?
6. Who is affected by these assumptions and what impact do they have?

Organisational Discrimination

Organisational discrimination should be explicitly covered by the Equality Act 2010, but what might not be recognised is the impact of discriminatory service development, e.g. restricting funding towards costly but niche services, or raising thresholds for service access in order to reduce waiting lists or to make best use of resources. Another, more worrying trend is the nature of the job specification for practitioner psychologists, and how this might exclude certain people due to the nature of their disability and the inherent assumption that practitioner psychologists in the NHS need to be consumers of masses of information, juggling more service users than is safe, expecting quick thinking and a robust 'can do' attitude. Although the expectation that practitioner psychologists can be flexible thinkers and can work under pressure is fairly explicit, individual differences in how speedily we can accommodate this pace and pressure means some individuals may leave the profession or avoid it entirely, leading to a less diverse workforce. Such workforce issues lead to inequality in accepted applicants onto practitioner psychology training courses.

A diverse workforce

Turpin and Coleman (2015) discuss the challenges in recruiting a diverse population into clinical psychology training. The *English Survey of Applied Psychologists in Health and Social Care* (British Psychological Society, 2004) showed that only 6.8% of the workforce were 'non-white' in the 25–44 age group, dropping to 4% in the over 45 group. Only 7% of successful clinical psychology applicants came from 'non-white' backgrounds. The Division of Counselling Psychology of the British Psychological Society's report on widening access (2017a) showed that despite the popularity of psychology as an undergraduate degree subject to those of 'non-white' background, estimated to be 12–19% of undergraduates, the successful applicants don't represent the true breadth of ethnicity. Key recommendations identified by Turpin and Coleman (2015) include the following:

- Developing schemes to widen access.
- Raising awareness of psychology as a profession across black, minority and ethnic communities.
- Developing specific recruitment materials to encourage those from minority or disadvantaged groups to apply.
- Reviewing the selection process.
- Developing more flexible routes to training.
- Regularly monitoring the results of these recommendations.

Have such initiatives translated into more successful applications from people who identify with one or more minority background groups? The Clearing House for Postgraduate Courses in Clinical Psychology (www.leeds.ac.uk/chpccp/) provides diversity data for successful applicants. Table 6.1 shows data across key diversity areas for 2005, 2013 and 2020, which represents the earliest and more recent available data at the time of writing. In 2005, data was not collected on sexual orientation or religion.

There is a small downward trend in the percentage of dominant group members (apart from those who report that they have 'no religion' and individuals

Table 6.1   Dominant group (diversity) % data for successful applications to clinical psychology courses, 2005, 2013 and 2020

Group	2005	2013	2020
Female	85	85.8	83
Heterosexual/straight	Not stated	92.6	80
No dependants	94	92.8	94
No disability	96	92	83
No religion	Not stated	60.4	72
White	92	87.1	82

with no dependants from 2013 to 2020), which is somewhat positive. Are these percentages representative of dominant groups across the UK population? The 2011 Census figures (Office for National Statistics, 2016) show that 86% of the UK population are White, 51% of the population are female, and 27.9% of the population have no religion. According to the *Annual Population Survey* in 2019 (Office for National Statistics, 2019), 93.4% of male respondents and 93.9% of female respondents across the UK identified as heterosexual/straight (this information was not sought in the 2011 Census). According to the *Family Resources Survey 2016–17* (Department for Work and Pensions, 2018), in 2016–17, 22% of the working age population reported a disability. Despite these figures being somewhat similar to the percentage of successful clinical psychology applicants from minority groups, the heart of the matter relates to the following questions, and it is here that data is lacking:

- What is the interview offer success rate of people who identify with minority groups when applying for professional training in psychology?
- In what way does professional training in psychology challenge Eurocentric assumptions of family, society, symptoms of mental ill health and therapeutic interventions?
- How many graduates from minority backgrounds pursue postgraduate training in psychology in comparison to graduates who are not from minority backgrounds?
- How representative of minority backgrounds are psychology lecturers and teachers?
- What are the progression and retention rates of students from minority backgrounds?
- Does the focus on academic performance in postgraduate training courses in psychology exclude students from minority backgrounds?

It is not within the scope of this book to consider these questions here, but for those involved in service provision or training, such questions need to be addressed. It is also of note that the gender divide persists, in addition to the lack of diversity in religious belief in the psychology workforce. Although the data presented here only represents one psychology profession, clinical psychology, such questions need to be asked of all professions.

Societal Discrimination

Inequality towards certain cultural and diverse populations persists in wider society despite the acknowledgement and apparent acceptance of difference within government policy, social and healthcare policy, and the wider community. From the perspective of a practitioner psychologist, in what way should they challenge discriminatory practices originating from political and societal arenas? According to the BPS *Practice Guidelines* (2017b), a practitioner psychologist should be aware of stereotypes and assumptions that are made when thinking about culture and ethnic groups. The guidelines also describe the nature of such discriminatory practices, as listed below:

- The interchangeable use of the terms 'race', 'culture' and 'ethnicity' results in misinterpretations which reduce the impact of community approaches to inequality and the availability of services.
- Services tend to adopt a 'one size fits all' approach which lacks formal recognition of diverse needs. I would expand on this and suggest that services should be flexible so as to encourage diverse approaches from practitioners (it seems that in trying to ensure equality, flexibility has been sacrificed).
- There is a lack of culturally relevant psychological therapies that go beyond Western ideologies and psychological theory. An example would be randomised controlled trials of a therapeutic approach with a non-diverse participant sample or tests that have been validated with a non-diverse sample.
- Not only is there a need for interpreters during assessment, formulation and intervention with service users whose first language is not English, but an awareness of the impact of culture, ethnicity and religion is also lacking. This is true of research in areas other than psychological intervention (as mentioned).
- Socially conditioned prejudice towards difference needs to be directly challenged.
- Models of mental health which are based on Western constructs need to be re-examined and amended to incorporate other views of psychological wellbeing.

The culturally competent practitioner

To truly understand what is meant by 'cultural competence', we need to consider a definition of culture. In contrast to discrete categories of difference and diversity (gender, age, disability, sexual orientation, religion, race), a person's culture and belief system is somewhat unique and mostly hidden. Tribe (2014) suggests that culture is not a discrete entity that is dependent on our place of birth, although where we live, in addition to ethnicity, race and religion, may shape our cultural values. Tribe further states that to live in a culturally diverse society means living in a dynamic system which is continuously shaped by new ideas, values and technologies, and our family, experience and interpretation of these. When considering what this means for the culturally competent practitioner, according to Kirmayer (2012), the aim is to make healthcare services more accessible, acceptable and effective for culturally diverse populations, through a competent system of behaviours, attitudes and policy that ensures the delivery of services to those in need. In a booklet produced by the Division of Counselling Psychologists entitled *Race, Culture and Diversity* (British Psychological Society, 2017a), the authors point out that, in attempting to engage with culture and diversity, there is a risk of perpetuating unhelpful behaviours and attitudes, and potentially causing harm.

Cultural Competence

According to the Division of Counselling Psychologists, in their publication entitled *Race, Culture and Diversity* (British Psychological Society, 2017a), to be a culturally competent practitioner is to understand that:

- Culture is dynamic.
- There is therefore no central definition of culture.
- Cultural knowledge and learning should be continuous.
- Culture can offer a template for recovery and is crucial for the purpose of the therapeutic relationship.
- Culture is an expression of experience and is not language-specific.
- It is unethical to lack awareness of cultural issues and diverse group experiences.

Challenging Discrimination: Intervention and Educational Approaches

Many organisations (not just health and social care) rely on intervention/educational training packages to combat discrimination in the workplace. An article by Hayes, Taylor and Oltman (2020) discusses the utility of current training approaches that aim to reduce harassing or discriminatory behaviour. They discuss the limitations of interventions that don't fully conceptualise the target problem correctly, are poorly designed and demonstrate a poor understanding of the psychological principles of attitude and behaviour change. They suggest a scientist-practitioner mindset when approaching training that addresses discrimination, incorporating accurate, theory-driven content and robust evaluation in order to see whether the training is effective. To measure effectiveness, there needs to be a clear definition of what outcomes are to be targeted. Hayes and colleagues (2020) provide an example of training provided by the company Starbucks, a chain of coffee shops, in response to an incidence of racial discrimination. In May 2018, 175,000 employees received a form of unconscious bias training (UBT) that was designed to overcome implicit bias, encourage conscious inclusion and prevent discrimination. The intended outcome was to uphold the values of 'humanity and inclusion'. As noted by Hayes and colleagues, is it possible to define and measure 'humanity and inclusion' as an evaluative outcome of the training?

Unconscious bias (UB) (also known as implicit bias) is considered to play a significant role in workplace discrimination (McGregor-Smith, 2017). According to Atewologun, Cornish and Tresh (2018), UB is defined as those attitudes we hold that we are unaware of and which are automatically activated, operating outside conscious awareness and influencing our behaviour. Unconscious bias training (UBT) involves taking a computer-based response test (such as the Implicit Association Test) that identifies unconscious associations made by the person towards target stimuli relating to discriminatory biases (e.g. straight people are good). By the speed with which a person presses a key, the strength of that association is thought to indicate their belief system. Noon (2018) puts forward a highly critical viewpoint of UBT in order to encourage debate about the utility of such training in reducing implicit bias. Is it any better at educating, influencing attitudes and impacting behaviour than more traditional pedagogical approaches? Is UBT's focus on personal limitations and avoidance goals a barrier to change (Tia Moin & Van Nieuwerburgh, 2021)? Clearly, there are problems with current iterations of training that aim to combat discriminatory practices, with research in the area showing conflicting results. While it is impossible to cover the range of UBT interventions or educational packages that is available here, the central message for the practitioner psychologist is the need for curiosity and adopting a critical stance.

What can practitioner psychologists do?

The following are suggestions that are designed to make you think about how a practitioner psychologist may work in this area. There are certainly groups forming across society to combat discrimination in its various forms, but our personal judgement and assumptions are our own, and we are responsible for our own interpersonal and organisational relationships.

- Areas to explore include assumptions and practices that could create barriers to anti-discriminatory practices. There should be a conscious effort to talk about and welcome diversity in all its forms. As practitioner psychologists, we are trained as communicators and leaders, and these skills can be used here.
- As scientist-practitioners, we have the skills to conduct research on behavioural interventions that challenge discrimination, and to identify measurable constructs that test the efficacy of such interventions.
- Any research should have inputs from a diverse population, representing all the groups it aims to help. Questions should be asked about what is the best way of challenging discrimination in our communities (not just at work, but beyond the workplace). Is it through education or intervention, or should it be based on communities coming together to learn about one another?

Summary

Many of us have attended equality and diversity training within our professional lives, and it typically involves education about the protected characteristics and types of discrimination. This is a good starting point, but taking legal action against discriminatory transgressions is not an easy task and can be time-consuming and expensive. As practitioner psychologists, we have the skills of a scientist-practitioner and can use these skills to explore issues of discrimination in therapy and in the wider work and societal context.

According to professional guidelines (Health and Care Professions Council, 2016; British Psychological Society, 2017b), we must not discriminate against others and discrimination should never affect service provision. It is also stipulated that we must challenge our colleagues if we believe they have behaved in a discriminatory way. It is impossible to create a set of 'one size fits all' guidelines, as doing so could remove the flexibility required to meet the needs of our diverse population and to identify areas where there could be improvement.

Discrimination in the form of micro aggressions are just as likely to happen in the context of the organisational setting or in multidisciplinary team work as they are in the therapy room. Practitioners need to be vigilant so that the underlying assumptions can be identified and addressed. Discriminatory behaviour can also be displayed by the service user towards the practitioner, and this can be a particularly challenging set of circumstances. Suggestions are made on how to respond to such a situation, but again, this is open to interpretation and will be influenced by the practitioner's individual circumstances.

As practitioners, we must continually challenge our automatic assumptions, whether through engaging in reflective practice and/or talking about it in supervision.

A diverse workforce is one that represents a diverse population. Research suggests that minority groups are not well represented in practitioner psychologist training cohorts and this needs to be addressed. The training packages that aim to challenge discriminatory practice within workplaces, and by default in delivery of services, also need to be open to critique.

Key Points

- The Equality Act 2010 is a key piece of legislation that aims to protect people against discrimination in employment and as consumers of public and private services.
- Discrimination can be direct or indirect, and harassment and victimisation are prohibited by the Act.
- The legal test for discrimination is that it is demonstrated that a person is treated less favourably than another person because of a reason related to a protected characteristic.
- Anti-discriminatory practice for the practitioner psychologist needs to incorporate three elements: (1) interpersonal relationships, (2) organisational discriminations, and (3) challenging societal behaviour.

Practice Case Studies

Case Study 1

You are employed as a Health Psychologist who specialises in behavioural interventions and goal-setting for service users who wish to improve their health through diet and exercise. You work with a diverse population across a wide range of ages, gender, etc., and find you value the challenge your work entails. You are aware of equality and diversity issues, having recently undertaken mandatory training delivered by your organisation for all staff. You feel that this may have been a 'tick box' exercise, but you also value the opportunity to question your own practice.

A colleague has referred a person to you who has diabetes and is struggling with weight gain. The referrer makes explicit reference to the person's weight and uses the term 'fatty' when talking about them. While in the moment you do not directly challenge this comment, you are surprised at the attitude displayed by a well-respected colleague.

You talk about this situation in supervision and reflect on your colleague's poor judgement in using the term. You feel that, on reflection, this is the type of comment that you have heard more than once. You begin to feel that you can no longer ignore such comments, but you are struggling with how to deal with the situation. You don't want to become an unpopular member of the team.

Suggested questions

1. What could you have done in the moment when the term 'fatty' was used?
2. How might you adopt a leadership role in bringing this matter to the attention of the wider team?

Case Study 2

You are a female Counselling Psychologist who is a member of a mental health team working with adults as part of a local NHS trust. You enjoy your work and feel that you are a valued member of the team, having worked for that employer for the past 10 years. A recent session with a male service user who has been referred for therapeutic intervention due to difficult relationships with others, exacerbated by angry outbursts, has caused some concern.

Your formulation is based on the hypothesis that the service user is overly anxious in their relationships and demonstrates an anxious attachment style resulting from early childhood trauma involving a female family member. In recent sessions, you find that you are increasingly feeling uncomfortable as the service user often interrupts you and makes discriminatory reference to your gender, such as 'women are far too emotional to be doing this type of work'. You have not tackled this in session, as you are concerned that such a response would lead to a fracture in the therapeutic relationship and potentially an angry outburst.

Suggested questions

1. What support would most help you as a practitioner working in this situation?
2. How might you respond in session to these references to gender? What benefits could there be in 'calling this out'?

References

Atewologun, D., Cornish, T., & Tresh, F. (2018) *Unconscious Bias Training: An Assessment of the Evidence for Effectiveness.* Equality and Human Rights Commission. Research report 113. Available at https://www.equalityhumanrights.com/sites/default/files/research-report-113-unconcious-bais-training-an-assessment-of-the-evidence-for-effectiveness-pdf.pdf

British Psychological Society. (2004). *English Survey of Applied Psychologists in Health and Social Care and in the Probation and Prison Service.* Leicester: BPS.

British Psychological Society. (2017a). *Race, Culture and Diversity: A Collection of Articles* (Division of Counselling Psychology). Leicester: BPS.

British Psychological Society. (2017b). *Practice Guidelines*. Leicester: BPS. Retrieved from www.bps.org.uk/sites/www.bps.org.uk/files/Policy/Policy%20-%20Files/BPS%20Practice%20Guidelines%20%28Third%20Edition%29.pdf

Department for Work and Pensions. (1975). *Disability Discrimination Act (1975)*. London. HMSO. Available at https://www.legislation.gov.uk/ukpga/1995/50/contents (accessed: 2 February 2021).

Department for Work and Pensions. (1975). *Sex Discrimination Act (1975)*. London. HMSO. Available at https://www.legislation.gov.uk/ukpga/1975/65/enacted (accessed: 2 February 2021).

Department for Work and Pensions. (1976). *Race Relations Act (1976)*. London: HMSO. Available at https://www.legislation.gov.uk/ukpga/1976/74/enacted (accessed: 2 February 2021).

Department for Work and Pensions. (2018). *Family Resources Survey.* Available at https://www.gov.uk/government/statistics/family-resources-survey-financial-year-201617

Government Equalities Office. (2010). *Equality Act (2010)*. London: HMSO. Available at www.legislation.gov.uk/ukpga/2010/15/contents (accessed: 26 June 2021).

Hayes, T. L., Taylor, L. E., & Oltman, K. A. (2020). Coffee and controversy: How applied psychology can revitalize sexual harassment and racial discrimination training. *Industrial and Organizational Psychology, 13*(2), 117–136.

Health and Care Professions Council. (2016). *Standards of Conduct, Performance and Ethics.* London: HCPC. Available at: www.hcpc-uk.org/standards/standards-of-conduct-performance-and-ethics/

Kirmayer, L. J. (2012). Cultural competence and evidence-based practice in mental health: Epistemic communities and the politics of pluralism. *Social Science & Medicine, 75*(2), 249–256.

McGregor-Smith, B. R. (2017). *Race in the Workplace: The McGregor-Smith Review.* Available at https://assets.publishing.service.gov.uk/government/uploads/system/uploads/attachment_data/file/594336/race-in- workplace-mcgregor-smith-review.pdf.

Noon, M. (2018). Pointless diversity training: Unconscious bias, new racism and agency. *Work, Employment and Society, 32*(1), 198–209.

Office for National Statistics, National Records of Scotland, Northern Ireland Statistics, & Research Agency. (2016). *2011 Census Aggregate Data.* UK Data Service (June 2016 ed.). doi: http://dx.doi.org/10.5257/census/aggregate-2011-1

Office for National Statistics, Social Survey Division. (2019). *Annual Population Survey, 2004–2018: Secure Access* (data collection). (14th ed.). UK Data Service. SN: 6721, http://doi.org/10.5255/UKDA-SN-6721-18

Owen, J., Tao, K. W., Imel, Z. E., Wampold, B. E., & Rodolfa, E. (2014). Addressing racial and ethnic microaggressions in therapy. *Professional Psychology: Research and Practice, 45*(4), 283.

Peters, H. J., Schwenk, H. N., Ahlstrom, Z. R., & McIalwain, L. N. (2017). Microaggressions: The experience of individuals with mental illness. *Counselling Psychology Quarterly, 30*(1), 86–112.

Schmitt, M. T., Branscombe, N. R., Postmes, T., & Garcia, A. (2014). The consequences of perceived discrimination for psychological well-being: A meta-analytic review. *Psychological Bulletin, 140*(4), 921.

Sewell, H. (Ed.). (2012). *The Equality Act 2010 in Mental Health: A Guide to Implementation and Issues for Practice*. London: Jessica Kingsley.

Shelton, K., & Delgado-Romero, E. A. (2013). Sexual orientation microaggressions: The experience of lesbian, gay, bisexual, and queer clients in psychotherapy. *Psychology of Sexual Orientation and Gender Diversity*, *1*(S), 59–70. doi/10.1037/2329-0382.1.S.59

Shiles, M. (2009). Discriminatory referrals: Uncovering a potential ethical dilemma facing practitioners. *Ethics & Behavior*, *19*(2), 142–155.

Sue, D. W. (Ed.). (2010). *Microaggressions and Marginality: Manifestation, Dynamics, and Impact*. Hoboken, NJ: John Wiley & Sons.

Sue, D. W., Capodilupo, C. M., Torino, G. C., Bucceri, J. M., Holder, A., Nadal, K. L., & Esquilin, M. (2007). Racial microaggressions in everyday life: Implications for clinical practice. *American Psychologist*, *62*(4), 271.

Tia Moin, F. K., & Van Nieuwerburgh, C. (2021). The experience of positive psychology coaching following unconscious bias training: An Interpretative Phenomenological Analysis. *International Journal of Evidence Based Coaching and Mentoring*, *19*(1), 74–89.

Tribe, R. (2014). Race and cultural diversity: The training of psychologists and psychiatrists. In R. Moodley & M. Ocampo (Eds.), *Critical Psychiatry and Mental Health: Exploring the Work of Suman Fernando in Clinical Practice*. London: Routledge.

Turpin, G., & Coleman, G. (2015). Clinical psychology and diversity: Progress and continuing challenges. *Psychology Learning & Teaching*, *9*(2), 17–27.

Turpin, G., & Fensom, P. (2004). *Widening Access within Undergraduate Psychology Education and its Implications for Professional Psychology: Gender, Disability and Ethnic Diversity*. Leicester: British Psychological Society.

Unzueta, M. M., Knowles, E. D., & Ho, G. C. (2012). Diversity is what you want it to be: How social-dominance motives affect construals of diversity. *Psychological Science*, *23*(3), 303–309.

7

Reflective Practice

On reading this chapter you will:

- Understand that reflective practice embodies a range of methods and approaches
- Understand what reflective practice is and why it is important
- Appreciate that reflective practice is a specialised form of thinking that leads to learning from experience, expanding practitioner knowledge beyond what can be learnt from scientific enquiry
- Understand that the skill of 'thinking on one's feet' is reflecting in action and is an essential skill developed through professional practice experience
- Learn that a range of reflective models exists to aid the practitioner, but these are not 'recipies' that need to be followed to the letter; the process is intuitive and should be tailored to the individual
- Be aware that reflective practice needs to be practised with care and in a supportive environment where cultural values are considered

Introduction

A practitioner in health and social care will be more than familiar with the concept of reflective practice. It is central to the skillset required in these professions and every experienced practitioner will recall the inherent difficulty in understanding the 'how to' of practising reflectively and demonstrating this at an interview or in training. This therefore begs the question: how do we learn the art of reflection and why is it so complex? Russell (2005) notes that reflective practice is sometimes considered additional 'fluff' by students in professional practice training, illustrating a lack of understanding as to its intention and purpose. Definitions of reflective practice tend to focus on the act of reflection rather than on reflection in practice, which does little to convince those who are tasked with undertaking critical reflection.

Dewey (1933: 9) asserted that reflection involves 'active, persistent and careful consideration of any belief or supposed form of knowledge in the light of the grounds that support it and the further conclusion to which it tends'.

Thus, according to Dewey, reflection, at its core, is an active process where there is an intention to challenge what is known. Boud, Keogh and Walker (1985: 19) define reflection as 'a generic term for those intellectual and affective activities in which individuals engage to explore their experiences in order to lead to a new understanding and appreciation'. Here, Boud extends the idea of reflection as being necessary to challenge what we believe to be true so as to develop new knowledge. Others, such as Moon (2013), suggest that reflection is a method of problem-solving where the knowledge we seek is absent. Each definition has a different focus on reflection; all can be described as true, yet they illustrate the complexity of reflection.

Reflective practice, as a construct and activity, was introduced by Schön (1987), who applied reflection to professional practice as an approach to problem-solving and a tool for continued learning. One of the most influential ideas proposed by Schön is that real-world problems cannot be solved using a 'one size fits all' approach where a psychiatric diagnosis (as an example) leads to the application of a predetermined technique. Reflective practice is therefore the process that can overcome the issue of individuality. People are messy, according to Schön, and it is a point on which we can all agree.

We can therefore presume that, given the messiness of humanity and human experience, the act of reflective practice is difficult to define, to act upon, and to evidence. It is not, however, a reason to disregard the practice. What it gives us is the clear message that we should be doing *something* about the challenges we face in our professional decision-making. This chapter will place reflective practice in context and provide the reader with an understanding of critical reflective practice and its complexities. Rather than focus entirely on the theoretical and philosophical aspects, the chapter will focus on what reflective practice looks like in reality and propose practical ways forward.

A specialised form of thinking

Dewey (1933) identified reflection as a 'specialised form of thinking' which rises from a doubt or hesitation related to experience. Rather than rely on already-acquired knowledge, Dewey proposed that reflection could lead to new knowledge through the act of trying out new ideas. Thinking in such a way therefore becomes purposeful.

Reflection 'in action' versus reflection 'on action'

The process of reflecting in and on action stems from Schön (1987), and his ideas are often cited in subsequent works on reflective practice. Rather than focus on 'reflection', Schön firmly led the way on emphasising the *practice* of reflection. Again, discussion on what reflective practice entails leads to different areas of focus, leading to potential misinterpretations (Munby, 1989). At the very core of Schön's idea is the dichotomy that exists between professional knowledge and scientific knowledge, where the absence of scientific 'rigour' or an objective form of analysis leaves professional knowledge a forgotten entity. Of course, Schön's ideas are not without criticism, with issues raised about the absence of consideration towards contextual matters, the absence of reflexivity, ignoring reflection-before-action, and the fact that Schön's approach is potentially unachievable (Greenwood, 1993; Usher, Bryant, & Johnston, 1997; Boud & Walker, 1998; Moon, 2013). I would argue that the sheer simplicity of Schön's ideas are missed. Reflecting in and on action can be considered from a variety of viewpoints; this is not a problem but an opportunity for useful discussion.

As we have already discussed in Chapter 1, evidence-based practice requires there to be a dynamic relationship between scientific knowledge and professional knowledge, thus placing professional knowledge as a key practice requirement. According to Schön, professional knowledge is *developed* 'in action', that is, we learn by doing. If we consider this in more general terms, much of the child development literature shows the different mechanisms by which a child navigates the world and acquires knowledge through experience. It is therefore quite logical to consider Schön's ideas as simply an extension of this 'knowledge through experience', which was the initial idea put forward by Dewey (1933).

According to Finlay (2008: 3), Schön's view was that humanity is 'complex, unpredictable and messy', and that at the core of professional practice, the practitioner must be able to 'think on their feet' and react intuitively and creatively. This acknowledgement within the scientific literature can, of itself, support practitioners who suddenly realise after many years of training and practice that at no point does their learning and knowledge reach a point of saturation. The practitioner needs to be comfortable with not having an immediate answer and to be able to take a step back. This is where 'thinking on our feet' (or reflecting and responding in action) becomes an essential skill, and one that is developed not through gaining more scientific knowledge, but through continued professional practice. What this implies, though, is that there is no recipe book approach to engaging in reflective practice. Despite this, many models have been developed to aid the practitioner in their reflection, but they should be considered as props rather than definitive guides.

Models of Reflective Practice

Reflective practice is a cornerstone of many different professions, and a number of 'models' have been created to illustrate the cycle of learning and reflection. Even though the models described below originate from a range of professions, including nursing and education, they are applicable across all health and social care professions. While they are merely tools to aid the practitioner, it is useful to explore and critique them when considering approaches to developing an effective reflective practice.

Kolb (1984)

Similar to the ideas of Dewey (1933), and thereafter Schön (1987), Kolb (1984) proposed that discovery from experience leads to learning. Kolb proposed a four-stage learning cycle termed 'experiential learning'. Stage 1 is 'concrete experience', where the event/experience has occurred. Stage 2 is 'reflective observation', where reflection takes place. Stage 3 involves 'abstract conceptualisation', where the individual learns from the experience, and Stage 4 leads to 'active experimentation', where an individual tries out what they have learned. This model does not directly explain the process of reflection, but firmly places the act of deliberate reflection as a learning process.

Gibbs (1988)

Extending the 'learning cycle' proposed by Kolb (1984), Gibbs (1988) proposed a 'reflective cycle' with the aim of helping practitioners work through an activity or experience systematically. Again cyclical, this model involves six stages and acknowledges prior learning, with the aim of building on this knowledge to develop clinical skills. The six stages are as follows:

- Description – recollection of events
- Feelings – recollection of reactions to events
- Evaluation – weighing up the positive and negative outcomes
- Analysis – exploring the evidence base
- Conclusion – what has been learnt
- Action plan – what can happen next time.

Of note is the absence of the stage 'reflection', which implies that the six-stage process encompasses the process of reflection.

Johns (2000)

Somewhat similar to Gibbs (1988), Johns' model of structured reflection asks a series of questions to elicit reflection on a particular professional experience. These are:

- Description – what happened?
- Reflection – what was the aim and what was the outcome?
- Influencing factors – what affected decision-making?
- Evaluation – what could have been done better?
- Learning – what will change in your future practice?

The reader would be forgiven for thinking that the models are variations on the same theme – that an event leads to re-evaluation and therefore learning. It is upon this central idea that reflective practice is based, as noted earlier in the chapter. However, such prompts or descriptive cycles fail to truly capture the depth of thinking necessary to engage in what is termed *critical* reflective practice (more on this later). Indeed, the use of such models seems to be limited to professional education, where they offer a useful structure upon which to teach and to assess the reflective practice skills of the student. Although a checklist of this kind can be a basic starting point when beginning the discussion on what reflective practice is, by continuing to rely on this surface level of thought the practitioner fails to draw on and develop their own intuitive approach, recognition of values and practice, and personal goals. As Schön noted, humanity is messy, and this not only applies to our service users but also to ourselves.

A question posed by Middleton (2017), a nurse academic, asks what other methods are available to the practitioner when the use of reflective practice models fail. Middleton reflects on her own journey and her dissatisfaction at being limited to a fixed path in order to achieve desired results. With great insight, she acknowledges the practitioner's ability to facilitate change in others through therapeutic practices within various contexts and the irony of not being adept at applying the same principles to her own learning and development. What was found to be missing was the opportunity to critically reflect.

Critical reflection

If we first consider what 'critical reflective practice' is in its most simple form, it is to question the thoughts, assumptions and actions that form the basis of our professional development (Fook & Askeland, 2007). To extend this further, we create a critical dialogue not just with ourselves, but outwardly. The notion of dialogue is one we shall return to later. It is not to be confused with 'critical analysis', which is the cornerstone of academic writing, where research outcomes or theoretical ideas are the focus of scrutiny. Fisher (2003) describes critical reflection as a set of higher-order thinking skills which target assumptions, values and beliefs that inform practice. Critical reflection adds a further layer of moral and ethical considerations onto reflective practice, something which is often omitted from traditional models of reflection. It also places reflection firmly into historical, cultural and political contexts.

This chapter does not aim to cover the philosophical traditions of critical reflection, which are varied and complex and unnecessary for our discussion here. What is more useful is to place critical thinking within the contexts already mentioned. Smith (2011) provides a useful model of critical reflection which encompasses four domains:

1. Personal: thoughts and actions – the recording of self-perception of reactions and behaviours.
2. Interpersonal: interactions with others – the examination of interpersonal interactions.
3. Contextual: concepts, theory and methods – questioning current knowledge.
4. Critical: political, ethical and social contexts – exploring issues of power.

Fook and Askeland (2007) describe how their process of critical reflection involves small peer groups of social work students or professionals. As a group, they reflect on 'critical incidents', i.e. examples of practice that were significant for the practitioner. Group members act as peer reflectors, offering guidelines and question prompts as an aid to critical reflection. Such prompts could incorporate the four domains outlined by Smith (2011). The use of such prompts in peer groups of this kind, according to Fook and Askeland (2007), can and do lead to transformative change.

Also of note are cultural norms, which can differ greatly when considering the notion of personal privacy. Brookfield (1995) describes three types of organisational and professional culture that can block traditional approaches to critical reflection and how we communicate that critical reflection. These are cultures of silence, individualism and secrecy. An organisation may also be rule-governed and target-driven, where there are limits on time allowed for continuing professional development activities, and particular professions may value scientific knowledge over process-informed approaches. The recognition of these cultures can inform critical reflective practice and, in doing so, can challenge long-held organisational and professional assumptions, which may then be subject to necessary change.

Reflexivity

Critical reflection involves 'reflexivity', which can be described as a process where knowledge creation and the self are interrelated. Mainly seen in the literature on research methods and the reduction of bias, reflexivity is an important part of critical reflection as it acknowledges that knowledge is socially constructed (as in the constructivist tradition; Smith, 2011). What distinguishes 'reflexivity' from the terms 'reflection' and 'critical reflection' is the 'self', i.e. critical self-reflection. According to Finlay and Gough (2003), there exists a continuum between reflection, critical reflection and reflexivity. It is a bridge between the experience (e.g. 'what happened') and the self.

The dark side of reflective practice

According to Smith (2011), the use of personal forms of critical reflection can lead to cynicism towards the self, isolated thinking and becoming too focused on ourselves. Smith goes further and points out the risk of critical reflection in education, where students create reflective journals which could potentially lead to a personally negative stance and self-criticism. It is therefore essential that educators emphasise the balance that exists between recognising our strengths and being aware of areas of weakness. Many of the issues described as the 'dark side of reflective practice' focus on student professionals, who at the beginning of their career are tasked to develop, and be assessed on, critical reflective practice.

As noted by Boud (1999), there are certain traps that can derail the critical reflector:

- Recipe following – using reflective models as a process of steps to achieve a reflective stance.
- Reflection without learning – unstructured time to reflect, lacking purpose.
- Intellectualising reflection – making reflection a purely cognitive process.
- Inappropriate disclosure – personal disclosure beyond what is appropriate.

The first three traps are straightforward and can be guarded against simply by acknowledging them. Of more concern, though, is inappropriate disclosure, which can seriously impact not only the practitioner's practice, but also their mental health and wellbeing. Self-disclosure has been covered extensively in the professional literature, where revealing one's own experiences can be discouraged (Fook & Askeland, 2007). This might be self-evident when conducting therapy, but when asked to reflect on an experience within their profession, at its core is an expectation that the individual considers their own personal experiences and the impact of that experience on current professional practice. Particularly risky is pressure felt by students on professional courses to disclose everything so that they receive a good mark (it must feel as if their career depends on it!).

When faced with the difficulty of engaging in critical reflective practice, a student may well reach for familiar problems that are negative; highlighting good practice requires self-confidence and it takes time and experience to be able to recognise and acknowledge what we do well. The assessment of critical reflection as part of educational course requirements may force students to face issues that they are not ready to face. At no point would we require a service user to disclose personal information that they were not ready to disclose, with the threat of losing their chance at therapy or fracturing the therapeutic bond. The ethical issues here are vast.

Regarding ethical concerns, we must also question certain rights that the student has, such as confidentiality, privacy and informed consent. With greater emphasis being placed on critical reflective practices within professional education, and the compulsory assessment of these practices, there seems to be little choice in whether a student or trainee is able to choose to engage in these course components, and if not, whether they are penalised for not doing so. Indeed, there does not seem to be any explicit informed consent process where the student is given a choice about engaging in critical reflection or information on what it could mean for them.

Students and practitioners may also feel that critical reflection is a means to expose incompetence (linking 'critical' with the 'negative'), which they may perceive as leading to negative consequences rather than as a learning opportunity. If we are to learn from our experience, then we need to explore our strengths and weaknesses in a safe place. This then begs the question, with whom and where does such a safe place exist? We may explicitly emphasise confidentiality within therapeutic sessions, but is this routinely done in supervision sessions or in peer group reflection? It takes a great deal of self-awareness and professional confidence to engage in meaningful critical reflection and to enter a dialogue with another person about our own critical reflection.

Skills underpinning critical reflective practice

Atkins and Murphy (1993) give a useful overview of the skills required for critical reflection. In addition to such skills, Atkins and Murphy highlight that when engaging in critical reflection, we must be open-minded and motivated, which are not skills in themselves but which should underpin critical reflective practice. The skills outlined are as follows:

- Self-awareness – the ability to recognise and analyse feelings.
- Description – the ability to communicate (verbally and in writing) details of the experience in addition to recalling an accurate memory of the key details.
- Critical analysis – recognising the relationship between assumptions and knowledge (see section on critical reflection).
- Synthesis – incorporating new knowledge into previous knowledge (developing new perspectives).
- Evaluation – judging the value against known criteria or standards.

You will note that this list of skills is similar to the models of reflection described earlier. The key difference here is that we are discussing 'skills' rather than 'steps' or 'activities' to engage in. More importantly, viewing the nature of critical reflection as engagement in a set of skills allows a more logical approach for the student or qualified practitioner, where the focus is on improving the skill (i.e. engaging in the practice) as opposed to improving critical reflection (which is a far more difficult proposition).

In any research activity or therapeutic practice, 'description', 'critical analysis', 'synthesis' and 'evaluation' are key skills. The one key skill that may be more challenging for the practitioner is 'self-awareness'. Novack, Epstein and

Paulsen (1999) focus on medical care and education but give a useful overview of the central components of self-awareness. To develop self-awareness, practitioners need to:

- Understand their psychological strengths and emotional weaknesses.
- Understand how their personality impacts on their relationships with others, e.g. their need for perfection.
- Be able to identify their assumptions, beliefs, values.
- Be aware of issues of family, race, class, culture and gender that might influence their reactions to others.
- Be aware of the differences between sympathy and empathy and the factors that influence their ability to display empathy rather than sympathy.
- Be aware of their stance towards paternalism, autonomy, benevolence, non-maleficence and justice.
- Recognise and acknowledge feelings such as love or anger towards certain service users.

Perhaps a focus on self-awareness rather than 'practising' reflection is a more appropriate starting point for educational programmes, and assessment should focus on these factors before entering the confusing realms of determining learning outcomes which lead to critical reflective practice.

Mindfulness

Although I am not a mindfulness practitioner, I do see a useful pairing between being mindful and self-awareness with regard to critical reflective practice. Actively seeking knowledge as opposed to unfocused attention inhibits creative insights and 'a-ha' moments (Webster-Wright, 2013). Rather than chasing knowledge, it may be more useful to sit back and allow such insights to occur naturally. As noted by Webster-Wright, engaging in critical reflective practice does not give us the definitive answer to all the difficulties we face. It does, however, remind us that clearing a space in our mind is possible, and is worth pursuing.

Reflective writing

A method of critical reflection that is often referred to and engaged in within educational establishments is reflective writing. This can be via diaries (Love, 1996) or reflective learning journals (Moon, 2013). Sutton, Townend and Wright (2007) identified the following benefits, which were elicited from cognitive behavioural psychotherapy students who took part in a series of focus groups on the topic of reflective learning journals:

- Reflective writing is a cathartic experience.
- It increases self-knowledge.
- It increases empathy with service users.
- Repeated reading of a reflective learning journal leads to a 'deeper' level of learning.
- It is a record of positive experiences or insights.
- It is a way of dealing with challenging and difficult experiences.

Sutton and colleagues (2007) also identify negative outcomes. Study participants found that the requirements of what was expected in the reflective learning journal was ambiguous across course lecturers and that this felt threatening. Participants called for explicit information on the aims, rationale, method of self-reflection and marking criteria prior to engaging in the task. Study participants also questioned how such a reflective learning journal could be marked given the subjective nature of the content. This interplay between wanting a specific guide and boundary is in direct contrast to having the space within which to be creative. Increasing the boundaries reduces the creative edge. This again brings into question the validity of professional course requirements which require the compulsory assessment of critical reflection.

It is therefore important to acknowledge the need for a structured and supportive facilitation of reflective practice within education and health and social care settings. Such support is essential to protect against the barrage of emotions that reflective processes elicit (Bennett-Levy et al., 2001; Bolton, 2010). It may not therefore be a question of whether critical reflective practice should be taught and/or assessed as part of professional education, but rather that a more sensible approach is needed in order to teach the skills (particularly self-awareness) explicitly or to facilitate such learning within a safe learning environment and then to illustrate how these components make up what we call critical reflective practice.

Spalding, Wilson and Mewborn (2002) note the value of reflective journals over other methods that are used to facilitate critical reflective practice. Spalding and colleagues state that the benefits of journals include having a permanent record of thoughts and experiences, that journals, when shared, are a means of establishing relationships with instructors (or supervisors), that journals are a safe outlet for personal issues and concerns, and that journals can aid our internal dialogue. Equally, it was found that a dialogue between the person engaging in critical reflection and the mentor was of most value. Such a dialogue seems to elicit greater clarity in our thinking, in much the same way as it does within therapeutic relationships with service users – it is this feedback that can truly inform our thinking and self-knowledge.

Feedback: A dialogue of critical reflection

It seems that for us to get the most out of our critical reflection, we need feedback in some form or another. Feedback sources in health and social care settings include self-evaluation, service user feedback, peer review and professional supervision. When considering the myriad techniques used in critical reflective practice, we should also consider how feedback can aid our self-awareness, particularly as it is argued in this chapter that a focus on self-awareness is a far better and more logical option. Smith (2011) outlines several reflective techniques whereby self-evaluation or other sorts of feedback can be built upon:

- Reflective writing (journals, diaries, memos, notes, critical incidents/ portfolio).
- Reflective summaries (tabulation/lists, feedback/self-evaluation).
- Diagrammatic representation (concept maps, mindmaps, conceptual diagrams).
- Creative representation (pictures, images, stories, video, film).
- Perspective-taking (stakeholder/service user views, reflective interview).
- Interaction (peer/group discussion, problem-based learning, service user teaching).

Cantillon and Sargeant (2008) state that feedback can lead to behaviour change and modification, yet when done poorly, or with a focus on the negative, it can result in poor motivation and performance. It is therefore not simply a matter of giving an opinion; it needs to be a measured response with the aim of becoming part of the critical reflection process. This highlights certain issues about responding to self-evaluation and service user feedback. As individuals, we may not be motivated to push our own boundaries or to challenge ourselves; equally, a service user may well feel uncomfortable stating their honest viewpoint given the power differential between them and the practitioner, or they may have difficulty with their own level of self-awareness. Of course, that is not to say that our colleagues or clinical supervisors/educators are without their own barriers to self-awareness or difficulty in challenging their peers/ students. So overall, it is a risky business but one that is worth the effort if we can truly challenge ourselves, our practice and our professional development.

With that in mind, it would be prudent to review what is considered good feedback practice. Although aimed at higher education, Nicol and Macfarlane-Dick (2006) provide seven principles of good feedback practice. The relevance, of course, is that critical reflection aims to elicit self-regulated learning and development in the same way that higher education does. As Nicol and Macfarlane-Dick (2006) note, feedback is not merely a cognitive technique, but a process that is inherently linked to motivations and beliefs.

The principles of good feedback

The seven principles of good feedback:

- Clarifies what expected performance is (against goals, standards, etc.).
- Begins or helps to reinvigorate the process of self-assessment.
- Shares pertinent information to the practitioner about their practice.
- Encourages a dialogue on critical reflective practice.
- Promotes positive beliefs about motivation and can improve self-esteem.
- Helps to identify gaps between current and desired performance.
- Gives the person providing the feedback the opportunity to explore their own methods in supporting critical reflective practice.

When considering each of these principles, we see the importance of accessing good sources of feedback (including oneself). It is an active process, which is also time-consuming. This is unfortunate as its value cannot be understated.

Summary

Having acknowledged the challenges of defining reflective practice, it would be logical to presume that a written account of how reflection can be applied to professional practice is somewhat redundant given its complexity. However, for most health and social care professions, professional governing bodies demand that such critical reflection takes place (to be discussed in Chapter 3). At its core, the primary goal of critical reflective practice is to continually question our professional activity, monitor our values, and change our practice where necessary. Although there are models and guides on 'how to' practise critical reflection, a wholly coherent approach is missing. It may seem like an impossible task to bring this together, but the contextual aspects of our work and lives provide much of the opportunity to engage our reflective activity. Clinical supervision is the space where psychological practitioners can engage in overt critical reflection, yet supervision is time-limited and may be taken up by more pressing, practical matters (active reflection on practice is challenging and time-consuming!). We can also reflect in our therapeutic sessions with service users, with our colleagues, and with ourselves using the techniques we have discussed in this chapter.

Rather than focus on what reflective practice should look like, it may be more sensible to consider what opportunities exist for this important task to take place. What level of importance do organisations place on reflective practice? Is it a nod in the right direction by mentioning it in the person specification document of job adverts, or is there a concerted effort by the organisation to offer space (psychological and physical) and time for critical reflection to occur? How many of us have put aside time in our diaries for this important task? Once we have this space and time, our own critical reflection is made explicit, to ourselves and others. It is an essential part of our working lives and should be given the same gravitas as adhering to a certain dress code or attending compulsory training.

What then should occur in professional training? Critical reflection is already built into such academic contexts and is taught and assessed. The ability to reflect is something that is looked for in interviews for such training places. It is, however, no less challenging to define and deliver this type of teaching than it is to qualify in a certain profession and to engage in critical reflection as a professional requirement. As noted by Hussey and Smith (2002), is formalising critical reflection within such training undermining what it aims to achieve? Is this activity merely based on the assessor's world-view, thus ignoring the emerging professional expertise unique to the students (Leach, Neutze, & Zepke, 2001)? Again, the answer may lie in providing the space and time to critically reflect, without the constraint of models or learning outcomes. This should be purposeful and structured time though, as it would be easy to fall into the trap of 'reflection without learning' (Boud, 1999).

Reflective practice is necessary for our own professional development and personal wellbeing as well in improving outcomes for our service users. Rather than approaching critical reflection from a 'top-down' perspective, where we try to understand what critical reflection is and what it involves, it may be more logical to adopt a 'bottom-up' approach, where we focus on practice skills, particularly self-awareness. The development of self-awareness can be straightforward, as illustrated earlier in the chapter. Self-awareness can help us 'think on our feet'. If we know our triggers and our areas of strength, we can skilfully respond to any situation. We know what it is to be self-aware and that there are tools to help us, such as engaging in mindfulness practice. It is ironic that such effort is given in teaching and learning on how to engage in critical reflection, when explicit acknowledgement of the messiness of humanity tells us that a linear approach is not going to be straightforward. The more we delve into the detail, the less we focus on the bigger picture. Such focus on the detail is illustrated by philosophical debates on the topic. These may be interesting, but do not help the busy clinician in their day-to-day tasks.

Key Points

- Critical reflective practice is challenging to define and therefore difficult to practise.
- There are reflective practice models upon which to base critical reflection, but they are simplistic and miss the depth of thinking required.
- Reflective practice models should not constitute a recipe approach to critical reflective practice.
- Critical reflection involves higher-order thinking which targets assumptions, values and beliefs that inform practice.

- Reflective practice can pose dangers to one's self-concept and determining the right level of self-disclosure can be challenging.
- Rather than focus on 'doing' critical reflection, a starting point might be becoming more self-aware.
- Critical reflection can involve journalling and engaging in feedback with others. Both methods have shown positive results.

Practice Case Studies

Case Study 1

You are a trainee counsellor on a six-month placement with a Child and Adolescent Mental Health Service (CAMHS). The team you work with are friendly and very supportive. Your clinical supervisor has set up regular meetings with you and a supervisory contract has been put in place. Overall, things are going well.

As part of your course requirement, you have been asked to develop and deliver a workshop to a group of social workers on 'Childhood Trauma and Attachment Issues'. As this seemed a good opportunity, you agreed to do it, but it will be the first time you make a presentation to a group of qualified practitioners. Although you have some knowledge of the topic, you are unsure what to cover in the workshop.

You feel terrified at the prospect of undertaking such a task but are unable to voice your concerns to your supervisor, who has the final say on whether you pass the placement. You also have personal experience of childhood trauma, which is an added stressor, although you did receive counselling during your teenage years and have flourished since.

The workshop is due to take place two weeks from now.

Suggested questions

1. What critical reflective skills would help in this situation?
2. How would you tackle the boundaries around self-disclosure? What personal and professional risks could there be?

Case Study 2

You are a trainee Counselling Psychologist on placement with a local Adult Mental Health Team. As part of the course requirement, you are tasked with keeping a weekly reflective journal while on placement, which is an assessed piece of work.

Your supervisor is an experienced consultant Counselling Psychologist with whom you have a good working relationship. However, you have noticed that your supervisor has poor self-care skills and frequently seems overwhelmed with the amount of paperwork and meetings. You have begun to question whether their situation is negatively impacting on colleagues and potentially on service users. You have found the reflective journal particularly useful in documenting your feelings and concerns, as you feel you cannot bring this issue up in supervision. As a trainee, your supervisor determines whether you pass or fail the placement, and raising such a sensitive matter feels inappropriate given the difference in status between you.

Your supervisor is aware of your reflective journal and has offered to give you some feedback on your work. You have not had time to fully anonymise the journal before submitting it for marking, where you intended to refer to your supervisor as a 'colleague'. As a result, you have begun to question your stance on this issue; is withholding your concern a part of the problem?

Suggested questions

1. When considering the discussion in this chapter on the importance of feedback in critical reflection, how would those ideas fit this scenario?
2. Balance the risks in this scenario. What are the likely outcomes?

References

Atkins, S., & Murphy, K. (1993). Reflection: A review of the literature. *Journal of Advanced Nursing*, *18*(8), 1188–1192. https://doi.org/10.1046/j.1365-2648.1993.18081188.x

Bennett-Levy, J., Turner, F., Beaty, T., Smith, M., Paterson, B., & Farmer, S. (2001). The value of self-practice of cognitive therapy techniques and self-reflection in the training of cognitive therapists. *Behavioural and Cognitive Psychotherapy*, *29*(2), 203–220.

Bolton, G. (2010). *Reflective Practice: Writing and Professional Development*. London: Sage.

Boud, D. (1999). Avoiding the traps: Seeking good practice in the use of self-assessment and reflection in professional courses. *Social Work Education*, *18*(2), 121–132.

Boud, D., Keogh, R., & Walker, D. (1985). *Reflection: Turning Experience into Learning*. London: Kogan Page.

Boud, D., & Walker, D. (1998). Promoting reflection in professional courses: The challenge of context. *Studies in Higher Education*, *23*(2), 191–206.

Brookfield, S. D. (1995). *Becoming a Critically Reflective Teacher*. San Francisco, CA: Jossey-Bass.

Cantillon, P., & Sargeant, J. (2008). Giving feedback in clinical settings. *BMJ*, *337*, a1961.

Dewey, J. (1933). *How We Think: A Restatement of the Relation of Reflective Thinking to the Educative Process*. Lexington, MA: D. C. Heath.

Finlay, L. (2008). *Reflecting on 'Reflective practice'*. Practice-based Professional Learning Paper 52. Buckingham: Open University. Retrieved from www.open.ac.uk/pbpl.

Finlay, L., & Gough, B. (2003). Introducing reflexivity. In L. Finlay & B. Gough (Eds.), *Reflexivity: A Practical Guide for Researchers in Health and Social Sciences* (pp. 1–2). Oxford: Blackwell Publishing.

Fisher, K. (2003). Demystifying critical reflection: Defining criteria for assessment. *Higher Education Research & Development*, *22*(3), 313–325.

Fook, J., & Askeland, G. A. (2007). Challenges of critical reflection: 'Nothing ventured, nothing gained.' *Social Work Education*, *26*(5), 520–533. https://doi.org/10.1080/02615470601118662

Gibbs, G. (1988). *Learning by Doing: A Guide to Teaching and Learning Methods*. Further Education Unit. Oxford: Oxford Brookes University.

Greenwood, J. (1993). Reflective practice: A critique of the work of Argyris and Schön. *Journal of Advanced Nursing*, *18*(8), 1183–1187.

Hussey, T., & Smith, P. (2002). The trouble with learning outcomes. *Active Learning in Higher Education*, *3*(3), 220–233.

Johns, C. (2000). *Becoming a Reflective Practitioner*. Hoboken, NJ: John Wiley & Sons.

Kolb, D. A. (1984). *Experiential Learning: Experience as the Source of Learning and Development*. Upper Saddle River, NJ: Prentice-Hall.

Leach, L., Neutze, G., & Zepke, N. (2001). Assessment and empowerment: Some critical questions. *Assessment & Evaluation in Higher Education*, *26*(4), 293–305.

Love, C. (1996). Using a diary to learn the patient's perspective. *Professional Nurse*, *11*(5), 286.

Middleton, R. (2017). Critical reflection: The struggle of a practice developer. *International Practice Development Journal*, *7*(1). https://doi.org/10.19043/ipdj.71.004

Moon, J. A. (2013). *Reflection in Learning and Professional Development: Theory and Practice*. Abingdon: Routledge.

Munby, H. (1989). Reflection-in-action and reflection-on-action. *Current Issues in Education*, *9*(1), 31–42.

Nicol, D. J., & Macfarlane-Dick, D. (2006). Formative assessment and self-regulated learning: A model and seven principles of good feedback practice. *Studies in Higher Education*, *31*(2), 199–218.

Novack, D. H., Epstein, R. M., & Paulsen, R. H. (1999). Toward creating physician-healers: Fostering medical students' self-awareness, personal growth, and well-being. *Academic Medicine: Journal of the Association of American Medical Colleges*, *74*(5), 516–520. https://doi.org/10.1097/00001888-199905000-00017

Russell, T. (2005). Can reflective practice be taught? *Reflective Practice*, *6*(2), 199–204. https://doi.org/10.1080/14623940500105833

Schön, D. A. (1987). *Educating the Reflective Practitioner*. San Francisco, CA: Jossey-Bass.

Smith, E. (2011). Teaching critical reflection. *Teaching in Higher Education*, *16*(2), 211–223.

Spalding, E., Wilson, A., & Mewborn, D. (2002). Demystifying reflection: A study of pedagogical strategies that encourage reflective journal writing. *Teachers College Record*, *104*(7), 1393–1421.

Sutton, L., Townend, M., & Wright, J. (2007). The experiences of reflective learning journals by cognitive behavioural psychotherapy students. *Reflective Practice*, *8*(3), 387–404. https://doi.org/10.1080/14623940701425048

Usher, R., Bryant, I., & Johnston, R. (1997). *Adult Education and the Postmodern Challenge: Learning Beyond the Limits*. Florence, KY: Routledge.

Webster-Wright, A. (2013). The eye of the storm: A mindful inquiry into reflective practices in higher education. *Reflective Practice*, *14*(4), 556–567. https://doi.org/10.1080/14623943.2013.810618

8

Leadership

On reading this chapter you will:

- Understand what being a leader involves
- Understand the function, skill and process of leadership
- Appreciate your role as a follower
- Understand the complexity of engaging in leadership activities
- Recognise what activities constitute leadership behaviour
- Acknowledge the importance of leadership from an organisational and professional body perspective
- Understand self-leadership and how to cultivate its skills to achieve your goals

Introduction

Leadership, as a professional skill, is becoming an essential requirement in professional psychology training programmes and related job specifications (regardless of grade). Historically, most definitions and writing on leadership are from a business management perspective. This can be problematic when such thinking is applied to health care, where people are at the heart of the organisation and its motivation as opposed to financial gain. However, with greater recognition of this skill in psychology professions, there are far greater resources available on what this means in practice (Division of Clinical Psychology, 2010). On a global level, leadership is the model in which collective efforts are organised into a course of action. On a micro level, each and every one of us has skills in self-leadership, allowing us to meet our goals. Leadership also has a number of functions and, according to Cyert (1990), these are (1) organisational, (2) interpersonal, and (3) decisional. Simply, Cyert sees these functions of leadership as determining the structure of the organisation, identifying the humanity of that organisation, and putting together a decision-making structure that achieves that organisation's goals. Other writers have focused on the process of leadership. Heifetz and Heifetz (1994) wrote about the dynamics of leadership, focusing on the adaptability of leaders in the face of new challenges. They saw leaders as continual learners who asked questions of themselves and the organisation. The authors noted that leaders need to take an objective view, that they 'look from the balcony'. Does this then suggest that anyone can be a leader?

Different theories have been proposed to account for what makes a good leader, and these theories continually change to better accommodate the dominant ideology of the time. Many writers on the topic of leadership identify key 'styles' of leadership, based either on a leader's 'fixed' personality characteristics (also referred to as 'traits') or on a more interchangeable set of skills that can be developed through appropriate training.

Where there is leadership there must be a group of followers, and a leader can only exercise power with the permission of these followers. Of course, this dichotomy of leader and follower is not so distinct; we can all be leaders and followers at the same time, in different contexts. It is therefore not only important to consider leadership skills, but to also look at what it is to be a good follower, as our actions as followers can shape the appointed leader. As noted by Hogan and Kaiser (2005), good leadership leads to effective team performance and subsequent individual wellbeing, whereas bad leadership leads to the opposite. The same can be said of being a follower. When 'following' blindly, with no consideration of our own moral code or the potential for harm, we are allowing 'bad' leaders to exert power. Ultimately, the ability to lead and to follow as a practitioner psychologist, while maintaining our own personal values, is the focus of this chapter.

Leadership as a Professional Skill

When we view leadership as one of the core skills of the practitioner psychologist, it lies logically among the other chapters of this book. As a profession, working as a psychologist is all about relationships, whether this is between the psychologist and the service user, the psychologist as a member of a multidisciplinary team, or the psychologist and the organisation (e.g. the National Health Service). The training involves preparing and enhancing skills that the individual already possesses (otherwise they would not have progressed to professional training). Supervision can model leadership behaviour and provides a space in which to reflect on leadership skills. Leadership is about promoting the value of applied psychology, through research and practice, as well as undertaking the role of scientist-practitioner and adopting an evidence-based approach to practice. Leadership requires self-awareness, an ability to lead ourselves, to pursue our ethics and values. Indeed, it is in our continued learning that true leadership occurs.

Onyett (2012) highlights how becoming a 'leader' is perceived as a struggle in which there needs to be some progression, as in 'climbing a mountain'. However, Onyett argues against this, and other interpretations of the 'challenge' of leadership, by stating that leadership should be seen as an 'opportunity' for furthering and improving service delivery, improving the process and outcomes for service users, and increasing practitioner experience and wellbeing.

The qualities of leadership

Radcliffe (2010, as cited in Onyett, 2012) notes that being a leader requires the following:

- The ability to form effective relationships.
- A sense of curiosity and a keenness to explore options.
- The ability to identify opportunities and to prioritise these.
- The drive to take action.

These requirements of a leader demand a certain energy from the practitioner, and requesting these of any busy clinician might lead to quite the opposite outcome. It is important to recognise that practitioner psychologists already have these skills. As Onyett (2012) points out, the process of leadership parallels the process of becoming a skilled practitioner.

Theories of Leadership

Historically, it has been of great interest how some people become leaders and how they are able to influence a great many people. There is something intriguing and potentially threatening about people who can influence your values, morals and beliefs. In identifying how leadership works, the mystery surrounding how these individuals compel their followers is somewhat diminished, and there is comfort in knowledge. Equally, it is of interest how to identify effective leaders so that organisations can flourish under the control of 'a safe pair of hands'. In the 1950s, the 'Great Man' theory postulated that people were born leaders. This gave leaders an air of mystery and heroism. Note the use of gender in this epithet – leadership was historically seen as a male quality. While it is recognised that such opinions are no longer acceptable, it is still notable that in psychological professions, where women outnumber men, far more men are seen in clear leadership positions (Clay, 2017).

Contingency theories of leadership

Contingency theories of leadership focus on needs, behaviours and contextual factors, where a balance is sought between all three. According to these theories, effective leaders must understand the values and opinions of their followers, rather than assuming absolute authority. This enables productive dialogue with team members about what the group stands for and how it should progress towards its goals. From this theoretical stance, it is believed that no fixed set of personality or behavioural traits can ensure good leadership, as the success of the leader depends on an understanding of the context and the nature of the group they lead. It is important that the leader shapes the group's identity so that the aims of leadership seem to be an expression of that identity. Transactional and transformational leadership styles fall into the contingency theories of leadership.

Bass and Avolio (1993) propose a multi-factor model of leadership which distinguishes between (1) transactional leadership, which is managerial in nature, attending to the tasks required of the team/followers, and (2) transformational leadership, which inspires followers to change for the good of the team or organisation. Transactional methods rely on 'contingent reinforcement', where followers are encouraged by rewards or corrected by negative consequences. Bass (1985) further developed the idea of transformational leadership and proposed that the extent of transformation is determined by the extent of influence the leader can exert on the followers. Bass introduced four elements of transformational leadership: (1) idealised influence, (2) inspirational motivation, (3) intellectual stimulation, and (4) individual consideration (Bass & Steidlmeier, 1999). Bass describes leaders as sitting on a continuum between transactional and transformational forms of leadership. No matter where leaders lie on this continuum, there are defining moments which are transformational to a greater or lesser extent. It is these moments of transformation that truly inspire teams to change. It is also of note that transformation occurs not only for those who are led, but also for those who lead.

Four components of transformational leadership (Bass, 1985)

1. Idealised influence – followers are loyal and hold the transformational leader in high regard. The leader has high ethical and moral standards.
2. Inspirational motivation – transformational leaders use values and ideals to elicit enthusiasm and confidence in their followers.
3. Intellectual stimulation – transformational leaders value innovation and followers who challenge norms within the organisation.
4. Individual consideration – transformational leaders focus on followers' needs where the aim is growth through consultation and coaching.

Personality and contingency theories of leadership

Personality remains a key area of interest in the leadership literature and attempts have been made in exploring the relationship between trait-like characteristics and contingency theories of leadership (e.g. transactional and transformational leadership styles). Results are varied, though, and due to a range of methodological concerns in the measurement of leadership constructs, strong reliable links have yet to be made. In a meta-analysis of 26 independent studies conducted by Bono and Judge (2004), the five-factor model of personality (Costa & McCrae, 1992) was used as an organising framework to explore how personality relates to leadership styles.

A proposed framework of personality traits and leadership (Bono & Judge, 2004)

- Extroversion – positive and ambitious, individuals who score highly on extroversion scales generate enthusiasm and motivation among followers.
- Neuroticism – individuals who score highly on neuroticism scales would be unlikely to adopt a leadership position.
- Openness to experience – individuals who score highly on this trait would be more likely to demonstrate inspirational leadership, with a vision for the future of the organisation/team.
- Agreeableness – those who score highly on agreeableness traits are more likely to be role models because of their honesty and kindness to others.
- Conscientiousness – individuals who score highly on this trait are goal- and detail-oriented, leading to a commitment to reach goals through hard work and self-discipline, thus inspiring such traits in others.

Although the results of the meta-analysis by Bono and Judge (2004) show a weak relationship between personality traits and transactional/transformational leadership styles, there is also some evidence that personality traits contribute towards leadership. As an extension to the five-factor personality model, it may be useful to consider the extensive literature on the personality traits of charisma and narcissism and how they influence leadership.

Charisma

Charisma is a personality trait that dominates the leadership literature but is notably absent from the five-factor model of personality. Charismatic leadership has some commonality with the transformational leadership style, yet transformational leadership is a far broader construct (Bass, 1985). As much of the literature on leadership in health care notes the value of transformational leadership, the role of charisma in these settings should not be ignored. Individuals who are charismatic by nature are known to motivate their followers to achieve incredible outcomes (Sosik, Chun, & Zhu, 2014). Sosik and colleagues define charismatic leadership as being a mix of personal attributes and behaviour, contextual factors and an ability to influence follower opinions. Leaders who are charismatic tend to shine in crisis situations, where they use their dominance, confidence and visionary charm to ensure the best outcomes for followers. These singular events can induce incredible loyalty in followers who are willing to make personal sacrifices for the good of the cause (Sosik & Dinger, 2007; Sosik et al., 2014). Of course, having a charismatic approach to leadership does not always lead to ethical and moral outcomes. The power of charisma can result in leaders deceiving and exploiting followers for their own needs (Bass & Steidlmeier, 1999). As practitioner psychologists, reflective practice and supervision are key in recognising poor leadership behaviour.

Narcissism

Charismatic leaders are blessed with attributes that can make those who follow them blind to their flaws. However, those leaders who use their charisma to feed their own needs and self-interest can cause destructive outcomes for their followers and the organisation (Howell & Shamir, 2005). A personality trait that is often seen where individuals display a high level of charisma is narcissism (Rosenthal & Pittinsky, 2006). Narcissistic leaders have an extremely high sense of self-importance, confidence and charisma, which is fed by the admiration and loyalty of the followers they undoubtedly attract (Sosik et al., 2014). The definition of narcissism is: feelings of entitlement (overt/covert), needing constant attention and admiration, being dismissive of the views/beliefs of others, thinking they are better than others (APA definition; Sosik et al., 2014).

Sosik and colleagues (2014) describe narcissism as leading to deficits in self- and interpersonal functioning, and although successful in the short term, narcissistic individuals are unlikely to maintain their status over time (Rosenthal & Pittinky, 2006). Hogan and Kaiser (2005) reviewed the empirical literature on the topic of personality and leadership and illustrated two aspects of reputation (upon which status and leadership can be attained): (1) the bright side – social performance and how we are at our best, and (2) the dark side – what others see when we are at our worst. Hogan and Kaiser (2005: 176) note that the cause of leadership/management failure is typically due to 'dysfunctional interpersonal dispositions', which coexist with talent and social skills yet result in the failure to build a team, which is an essential task of leadership. Of course, such traits are typically masked initially by charisma and social skills, which are enough to put these individuals into powerful positions. According to Paulhus (1998), those individuals who are high on trait narcissism make such a strong initial impression that they are more likely to become the nominated leader, although group rejection occurs in time when the less attractive personality traits (the dark side) present themselves (Hogan & Kaiser, 2005).

This contrasts with 'productive narcissists', who pursue grand visions and innovations, where the impairments in self- and interpersonal functioning are buffered by self-awareness, self-knowledge and organisational boundaries (Kets de Vries, 2006). The potential positive relationship between charismatic leadership and narcissistic traits has been encapsulated in the study by Sosik and colleagues (2014), who found the following:

- A positive relationship between leader charisma and follower empowerment and moral identity.
- Follower empowerment is greater when followers perceive the more constructive narcissistic personality traits of the leader.
- Follower empowerment mediates the interaction between charisma and narcissism and moral identity.

What is apparent in the literature on this topic is that certain personality traits can result in easier access to leadership positions. This is highly dependent on the followers, who create the context and environment for leaders to thrive. Although certain 'dark traits' can have disastrous consequences for teams and organisations, initially the vision and innovations put forth by such individuals can have a positive impact on team effectiveness and organisational success. The power therefore seems to lie with those who are led, the followers.

The Follower

Leadership as a social process

Based on what has been written so far, leadership, as a social process between leader and follower, is therefore a compelling view of how leadership works. Ehrhart and Klein (2001) base their view of follower behaviour and leadership outcome as operating under the following evidence-based assumptions:

- Followers will differ in their responses to leader characteristics, regardless of the style of leadership.
- Followers prefer leaders who share their values and who will meet their needs.
- The beliefs held by followers on certain leadership styles will influence their acceptance of that particular style.
- Organisational outcomes are predicted by follower satisfaction with, and positive evaluation of, those who lead them.

Crucially, Ehrhart and Klein (2001) found that follower preference is influenced by the following values: extrinsic and intrinsic rewards, interpersonal relations, security and collective identity. Such values indicate a needs-led process of leader–follower relationship, and the authors conclude that it is follower values (in addition to personality traits) that shape follower preference for certain types of leader. Ultimately, from a professional psychology perspective, we need to be aware of our values (from reflection and self-awareness) in order to understand our relationship with those who lead us (team manager, organisational leads, supervisors, etc.). We also need an understanding of the values of those we intend to lead or influence as part of our professional role, and of how they may respond to different approaches.

Organisational and Professional Frameworks

The NHS Leadership Framework describes what good leadership looks like in the National Health Service. It was published on behalf of the NHS Leadership Academy (Storey & Holti, 2013). The Framework attempts to identify the core aims, and the associated outcomes, which can form a leadership model fit for the NHS. The proposed aims are:

- To provide and justify a clear sense of purpose and contribution.
- To motivate teams and individuals to work effectively.
- To focus on improving system performance.

The service user is clearly at the heart of these aims, and they certainly encompass the aims of a practitioner psychologist. The Division of Clinical Psychologists (DCP), a sub-group of the British Psychological Society, have gone further and have designed a specific Leadership Framework for the profession (Division of Clinical Psychology, 2010). It is designed to inform training curricula as well as professional and organisational programmes of continuing professional development. The document outlines the specific skills required of a Clinical Psychologist, from being a trainee to clinical director. A distinction is made between clinical skills, professional skills and strategic-level skills (i.e. those skills required at the organisation level). The DCP Leadership Framework identifies ways of developing these skills in addition to offering ideas about how these skills can be used.

It is crucial that practitioner psychologists emphasise their worth in large organisations such as the NHS, given the drive to disperse much of the therapeutic work to other, more cost-effective roles (e.g. psychological wellbeing practitioners). In promoting the profession as being key in responding to an ever-changing financial and political landscape, and in designing and delivering mental health services, its future as a profession is secured. As practitioner psychologists, we have a responsibility to recognise our individual leadership qualities and to maintain these qualities through continued leadership activity. You are advised to seek out current documents relating to leadership so that you know what is recognised as leadership activity. I would also argue that there should be an acknowledgement of such skills among seasoned practitioners so that these skills are recognised for what they are – leadership skills. Given the inherent parallel between the skills already demonstrated by practitioner psychologists and those skills identified as evidence of leadership, there is a danger that the recognition of that evidence is lost.

As noted in Chapter 2 on multidisciplinary team working, much of the work of a practitioner psychologist rests on collaboration with a range of other disciplines to achieve team and organisation goals. Although there will be a designated team manager, we have seen how there are organisational, clinical and professional demands for leadership skills from all team members. It is also true that teams that work well together produce better outcomes for service users (Corrigan & Garman, 1999). How, therefore, does leadership work in a team environment if the practitioner psychologist is not in a traditional leadership or management role? The answer lies in viewing leadership as a developmental skill rather than a fixed construct, where there needs to be a continual process of reflection, study and acquisition of experience (Jago, 1982).

If we consider the work of Corrigan and Garman (1999), they helpfully remind us that the characteristics of multidisciplinary teams are as follows:

- Development of relationships and good communication.
- Cooperation in executing interventions and treatment plans.
- Professional identity, which is formed by membership of that team.
- Having shared goals.

We can map these characteristics onto the *Clinical Psychology Leadership Development Framework* (Division of Clinical Psychology, 2010), which usefully outlines how leadership can be demonstrated in a multidisciplinary team environment. Table 8.1 gives some suggestions on how practitioner psychologists can exhibit leadership skills in multidisciplinary teams.

Table 8.1 shows what the practitioner does to demonstrate leadership within multidisciplinary teams and how this might happen. In individual teams, much depends on the team's culture and climate. According to Sharma and Jain (2013), each organisation has a distinct culture that is made up of a range of factors, including past and current leaders, team history, past events and size. These factors result in how the team operates, its rules, traditions and customs. The team climate is how it feels to be in that team or organisation. It is directly related to the leadership within the organisation. Whereas team culture may be challenging to navigate, the climate of the multidisciplinary team is far easier to influence.

Table 8.1   Exhibiting leadership skills in multidisciplinary teams

Team characteristics (Corrigan & Garman, 1999)	*Clinical Psychology Leadership Development Framework* (Division of Clinical Psychology, 2010)
Relationships and communication	Conflict management skills. Encouraging team reflection. Demonstrating emotional intelligence, assertiveness and negotiation skills. Using different psychological models to explore team functioning.
Cooperation	Contributing to team reflection. Contributing to the supervision, teaching and consultation of other team members and junior staff.
Professional identity from group membership	Applying psychological theory to shared care plans. Leading on psychological formulation. Advising directors/commissioners on speciality clinical standards in relation to team goals.
Shared goals	Evaluating service outcomes. Auditing self and fellow professionals. Inspiring and supporting team members to adopt creative solutions. Developing leadership skills in others.

Team climate

According to Sharma and Jain (2013), team climate depends on the following:

- Clarification of goals – what is expected of team members
- The system of recognition, rewards and punishments
- Leader competence
- Freedom to make decisions
- What happens when mistakes happen.

As a multidisciplinary team member, the practitioner psychologist has the skills and knowledge to directly impact perceptions within the team. If any of the noted climate factors are unclear, or impact the team negatively, the practitioner psychologist can work (in collaboration with the multidisciplinary team) to overcome these issues.

Self-leadership

This chapter has mostly focused on overt leadership behaviour, as demonstrated by those who have responsibility over others, and where collective efforts are organised into a course of action. It is also true that individual acts lead to a course of action that either meets the individual's needs or the needs of the team or organisation. This is termed self-leadership. Manz (1986) developed the initial theory of self-leadership and defined it as self-influence that leads the individual towards tasks that are either naturally motivating or those that are not but are necessary as part of the role.

Elements of self-leadership

According to Manz (1986), there are three crucial elements of self-leadership:

- It addresses standards for self-influence, i.e. questioning the rationale behind the goals set for the individual/team/organisation.
- It incorporates intrinsic work motivation, i.e. adapting the relationship/perception of tasks so that they are 'naturally' rewarding.
- It adds thought strategies for self-leadership practice, i.e. (1) adapting the work context (immediate environment, culture and climate) to make it more motivational, (2) recognising what is naturally rewarding in task processes so that activities (based on feelings of competence, self-control and purpose) can be adapted within the job specification for that role, and (3) focusing mental energy on the positive aspects of the job role, leading to greater motivation.

As a practitioner psychologist, it is expected that individuals take more responsibility for their own job role and task behaviour. Self-leadership demands the same, and, as noted by Houghton and Yoho (2005), involves strategies that are aimed at developing skills that lead to better performance and effectiveness. Within the profession, we have opportunities that enable self-leadership, such as supervision, reflection, continued professional development, and so on. It is also worth focusing on these opportunities while training and in the early stages of your career so that you can evidence self-leadership development should there not be wider opportunities available to do so. Those in supervisory roles can also adopt an approach that encourages self-leadership practices.

When considering the benefits of self-leadership more widely, Carmeli, Meitar and Weisberg (2006) highlight the beneficial aspects of self-leadership for the organisation. Carmeli and colleagues explored the role of innovation within the self-leadership model noted by Manz (1986), and found that such innovation leads to better functioning and outcomes for that organisation. They suggest that global leadership approaches encourage innovation in employees. The actual process of innovation involves a staged process where ideas/solutions are proposed for a known challenge, those ideas/solutions are promoted and sustained, and then adopted within the wider organisation (Carmeli et al., 2006). In encouraging such innovative practices, Andressen, Konradt and Neck (2011) found support for their hypothesis that individuals who practise self-leadership within a transformational leadership setting are better motivated. From a professional skills perspective, it is important that you explore your own leadership style and that you build your awareness of self-leadership, primarily identifying what you find motivating within your professional practice.

Summary

Leadership can be viewed from a global level where a group's collective effort becomes a course of action, whereas self-leadership adopts the same skills in order to achieve our personal goals in relation to our profession. Leadership can have different functions and adopt a range of processes. When considering leadership, we must also think about what it is to be a follower, and how this influences the power held by the leader. We are all leaders and followers in different contexts. Leadership may depend on the practitioner psychologist's personality, skillset or style, although it is clear that it is not one trait or overarching style that truly captures what it is to be a leader. Leadership is a process of continued learning and reflecting on experience, which can seem challenging, but you must remember that to be chosen to train as a practitioner psychologist means that you have the basic skills in place. More recent theories on leadership posit the continuum between a more transactional (managerial) style and a transformational (inspirational) style.

Regardless of style, leadership should be recognised as a unique professional skill so that the psychology profession can maintain its status within the NHS. Leadership is a skill that requires continued learning and development, whether the practitioner psychologist is in a managerial role or not. With personality traits such as charisma being a key factor in transformational leadership, we should not forget the other side of charisma – narcissism – and we should not assume that charismatic leaders can maintain their status over the long term. At its core, leadership is a social relationship between the leader and follower, and many factors can influence this relationship. No matter where you are in your career, it is crucial to develop self-leadership skills and to recognise these so that you can evidence your learning and development in this area.

What is apparent in this chapter is the breadth of traits and behaviours that are theorised as being key in making a great leader (or even a competent one!). It may be the charismatic individuals with whom we associate good leadership, who inspire great change, and are foremost in our minds when we consider what leadership is, but leadership requires a continued focus on the job at hand, something that charisma does not support (on its own). Although personality is weakly associated with the contingency theories of leadership, such as transactional and transformational styles, it is without doubt within our very nature to lead and to follow, guided by our individual differences. That said, there are numerous guidelines (Division of Clinical Psychology, 2010) which can inform us on 'how' to demonstrate leadership behaviour. This can then be clearly evidenced.

There seems to be a dichotomy between 'how' we lead and the 'outcomes' of our leadership activity. What is the measure of our success? Is simply engaging in and evidencing leadership behaviour enough, or do we need to evidence the outcome of that activity by looking at those who follow us? From a professional perspective, we should be careful of adopting a tokenistic approach to leadership so that we can progress in our roles. We should only engage in leadership behaviour that has clear (and necessary) outcomes for the organisation, the multidisciplinary team or the service user.

Key Points

- Leadership is not one type of personality, one style or one set of skills; we need to identify our own unique leadership approach that combines the most useful aspects of all three.
- We are all followers, and it is our voice and behaviour that allow those who lead to have power over us; as a practitioner psychologist, it is within our professional standards to challenge practices that are not in the best interests of others or that could breach the organisation's moral code and values or our therapeutic relationship with service users.
- To recognise and develop our own leadership skills can be challenging, and there is comfort in allowing others to be in decision-making roles; we must remember why we chose this profession and the challenges we welcomed as part of the role – we already demonstrate leadership and decision-making skills in our day-to-day work.
- In the absence of clear opportunities to overtly lead teams or peers, it is important to cultivate self-leadership skills so that these can be evidenced (and to make our working lives more satisfying).

Practice Case Studies

Case Study 1

You have been working as a Counselling Psychologist for over 10 years. You recently started working with a Child and Adolescent Mental Health team. You enjoy your work and thrive on the challenges it provides. You feel you have a good working relationship with your colleagues, who are a mix of social workers, mental health nurses and Clinical Psychologists.

You have been tasked by the team manager to set up links with local schools. You have been asked to deliver a presentation on mental health and wellbeing to the students of these schools and to support teaching staff on how to respond to students who present to them with mental health concerns.

Some headteachers are resistant to this input as they feel your service is requiring school teaching staff to respond to student mental health concerns when they do not have any training in mental health. You have faced negative responses from them, such as 'It is not our job' and 'We don't have time'. You find this resistance challenging and are therefore avoiding the issue. You focus your energy on the schools that are keen to engage and feel things are going well.

The team manager has requested a meeting with you to discuss your progress and you suddenly realise that you will have to admit that you have avoided consulting with some of the schools. It has been some months since you were given the task and you feel your professional integrity will be questioned.

Suggested questions

1. Who are the leaders in this case scenario? Who are the followers?
2. How can you overcome this issue using self-leadership?

Case Study 2

You have been working as a Health Psychologist at a local general hospital for two years, and it is your first job since qualifying. You are part of a team of social workers and are the only Health Psychologist. You have developed good working relationships with consultants and ward staff, who regularly refer patients to you.

Your role in the team is to help patients with psychological issues arising from chronic health conditions (e.g. problems with non-adherence to medication, helping them to cope with their diagnosis, etc.). The social workers you work with are friendly and you meet weekly to discuss referrals and upcoming discharges for patients referred to your team. Although your work is somewhat different from that of the other team members (social workers focus on discharge and ongoing care in the community), you often discuss patients and organisational issues.

You have noticed over previous months that many of the referrals made to the team have to wait longer than is appropriate and you are concerned that this has a negative impact on patient care. Team members appear overworked and unmotivated, and the team manager (who is a social worker) does not seem to address these issues.

Your supervisor, who is a more experienced Health Psychologist at another hospital, meets you on a monthly basis.

Suggested questions

1. In what way might follower behaviour be contributing to the situation described here?
2. What organisational and professional standards might inform your work in this case?

References

Andressen, P., Konradt, U., & Neck, C. P. (2011). The relation between self-leadership and transformational leadership: Competing models and the moderating role of virtuality. *Journal of Leadership & Organizational Studies, 19*(1), 68–82. https://doi.org/10.1177/1548051811425047

Bass, B. M. (1985). *Leadership and Performance beyond Expectations*. New York: Free Press.

Bass, B. M., & Avolio, B. J. (1993). Transformational leadership and organisational culture. *Public Administration Quarterly, 17*, 112–121.

Bass, B. M., & Steidlmeier, P. (1999). Ethics, character, and authentic transformational leadership behavior. *Leadership Quarterly, 10*(2), 181–217. https://doi.org/10.1016/S1048-9843(99)00016-8

Bono, J. E., & Judge, T. A. (2004). Personality and transformational and transactional leadership: A meta-analysis. *Journal of Applied Psychology, 89*(5), 901–910. https://doi.org/10.1037/0021-9010.89.5.901

Carmeli, A., Meitar, R., & Weisberg, J. (2006). Self-leadership skills and innovative behavior at work. *International Journal of Manpower, 27*(1), 75–90. https://doi.org/10.1108/01437720610652853

Clay, R. A. (2017, July). Women outnumber men in psychology, but not in the field's top echelons. *Monitor on Psychology, 48*(7). Available at www.apa.org/monitor/2017/07-08/women-psychology

Corrigan, P. W., & Garman, A. N. (1999). Transformational and transactional leadership skills for mental health teams. *Community Mental Health Journal, 35*(4), 301–312. doi: 10.1023/a:1018757706316.

Costa, P. T., Jr., & McCrae, R. R. (1992). *Revised NEO Personality Inventory (NEO-PI-R) and NEO Five-Factor (NEO-FFI) Inventory Professional Manual*. Odessa, FL: PAR.

Cyert, R. M. (1990). Defining leadership and explicating the process. *Nonprofit Management and Leadership, 1*(1), 29–38. https://doi.org/10.1002/nml.4130010105

Division of Clinical Psychology. (2010). *Clinical Psychology Leadership Development Framework*. Leicester: British Psychological Society.

Ehrhart, M. G., & Klein, K. J. (2001). Predicting followers' preferences for charismatic leadership: The influence of follower values and personality. *Leadership Quarterly, 12*(2), 153–179. https://doi.org/10.1016/S1048-9843(01)00074-1

Heifetz, R. A., & Heifetz, R. (1994). *Leadership without Easy Answers* (Vol. 465). Cambridge, MA: Harvard University Press.

Hogan, R., & Kaiser, R. B. (2005). What we know about leadership. *Review of General Psychology*, *9*(2), 169–180.

Houghton, J. D., & Yoho, S. K. (2005). Toward a contingency model of leadership and psychological empowerment: When should self-leadership be encouraged? *Journal of Leadership & Organizational Studies*, *11*(4), 65–83.

Howell, J. M., & Shamir, B. (2005). The role of followers in the charismatic leadership process: Relationships and their consequences. *Academy of Management Review*, *30*(1), 96–112.

Jago, A. G. (1982). Leadership: Perspectives in theory and research. *Management Science*, *28*(3), 315–336.

Kets de Vries, M. F. R. (2006). *The Leader on the Couch: A Clinical Approach to Changing People and Organisations*. New York: Wiley.

Manz, C. C. (1986). Self-leadership: Toward an expanded theory of self-influence processes in organizations. *The Academy of Management Review*, *11*(3), 585–600.

Paulhus, D. L. (1998). Interpersonal and intrapsychic adaptiveness of trait self-enhancement. *Journal of Personality and Social Psychology*, *74*, 197–208.

Radcliffe, S. (2012). *Leadership: Plain and Simple*. Pearson UK. As cited in Onyett, S. (2012). Leadership challenges for clinical psychologists: Challenge or opportunity? *Clinical Psychology Forum*, *238*.

Rosenthal, S. A., & Pittinsky, T. L. (2006). Narcissistic leadership. *The Leadership Quarterly*, *17*(6), 617–633.

Sharma, M. K., & Jain, S. (2013). Leadership management: Principles, models and theories. *Global Journal of Management and Business Studies*, *3*. Retrieved from www.ripublication.com/gjmbs.htm

Sosik, J. J., Chun, J. U., & Zhu, W. (2014). Hang on to your ego: The moderating role of leader narcissism on relationships between leader charisma and follower psychological empowerment and moral identity. *Journal of Business Ethics*, *120*(1), 65–80.

Sosik, J. J., & Dinger, S. L. (2007). Relationships between leadership style and vision content: The moderating role of need for approval, self-monitoring, and need for social power. *The Leadership Quarterly*, *18*(2), 134–153.

Storey, J., & Holti, R. (2013). *Towards a New Model of Leadership for the NHS*. London: NHS Leadership Academy.

9

Practitioner Resilience

On reading this chapter you will:

- Appreciate why psychology is an attractive career option for some
- Understand the 'cycle of caring' and what it involves
- Be able to appreciate the risk and hazards that face practitioners
- Understand vicarious trauma, compassion fatigue and burnout
- Understand the importance of self-care
- Acknowledge that resilience can be built upon challenges

Introduction

One of the first questions an aspiring psychologist is often asked at job interviews or during training programme interviews is 'Why do you want to become a psychologist?'. This is an interesting and problematic question as the answer that inevitably springs to mind is 'to help people'. Of course, the trick, as most people in the profession will advise, is to think of something original, something that will make you stand out among the crowd. Just take a few seconds to think about this ... you may find the task easy, or not.

While we do help people, there are other rewards in being a practitioner psychologist. The rewards of the profession can span our intellectual, emotional and spiritual being, and provide many benefits, such as professional and personal growth and success. Yet there is an integral paradox in the role. The work is also challenging, pushes us beyond our limits and terrifies us at times. The stories we hear and the people we meet will often lead us to the depths of sorrow and despair. We experience pain alongside those we support. What brings us joy, also brings sorrow. There are unique challenges in this therapeutic work, as outlined by Barnett, Baker, Elman and Schoener (2007):

- The emotional demands, such as therapeutic relationships that challenge our boundaries.

- Service users who do not improve, despite the best efforts of the psychologist (and service users who often relapse).
- Suicidal service users or those who commit heinous acts against themselves or others.
- Administrative and organisational demands.

The work can be exhausting, and dealing with crisis after crisis adds to the stressors that practitioners experience. As noted by Skovholt and Trotter-Mathison (2016), there is a demand for us to be attuned, to have an energy that maintains our motivation when working with an individual who is often defiant or hopeless. We do this time and time again, and we often risk projecting our own feelings onto the service user (Yalom, 2002) or experience the service user's feelings as our own. Our empathy is an essential component of our work, yet it can also mean that we are subject to the highs and lows presented to us in the therapeutic space. Skovholt (2005) proposed a model of the therapeutic process termed 'the cycle of caring'. It is based on the relational nature of therapeutic work, and emphasises that much of the success of any therapeutic contact is based on the quality of that relationship. The cycle identifies four stages of the practitioner–service user journey:

- Empathic attachment – developing an open and trusting relationship.
- Active involvement – the helping contract (what needs to be done).
- Felt separation – letting go of active involvement.
- Re-creation – moving away from the work.

Each of these stages is experienced over and over again with each service user. Without variation in service user contact, the cycle of caring can become onerous and lose its value for the practitioner psychologist. We will return to this point, but the question I pose here, and that is captured by Skovholt (2005), is how does the practitioner psychologist truly give their presence, offer the attachment that is needed, and then end this alliance before moving on to the next? Skovholt describes this ability as a professional skill, and it is one that I would argue is the most challenging to maintain.

This chapter aims to take you on a journey where you will be faced with the realities of practice, the hazards and potential trauma. We will discuss compassion fatigue and burnout. Yet it is not written with the aim of emphasising the negative; it is written to acknowledge that limits will be reached and self-care must be a priority. Building resilience is at the very core of any helping profession. And by the end of this chapter, you will see that personal growth is the fundamental attraction of such a challenging yet worthwhile profession.

Areas of Potential Challenge

Organisational challenges

We have discussed in other chapters how organisational practices can work against the practitioner psychologist, such as the demands of therapeutic case loads and timescales, and limitations of funding and resources, etc. This is particularly true for the day-to-day therapeutic work, and such barriers to professional practice can impact on practitioner wellbeing – as well as impacting on the service user, which typically adds to the stress on the practitioner psychologist. Frustration with the work environment and work practices that fight against the evidence base, service user needs and practitioner values can build up, and cause resentment that can diminish the practitioner psychologist's ability to carry out the cycle of caring. Chapter 2 on multidisciplinary team working offers some advice on how such situations can be challenged within a team environment. Developing leadership behaviours can also be helpful when calling for organisational change to ameliorate workplace challenges and stress.

The therapeutic relationship

The next area of potential hazard that the practitioner psychologist should be aware of is the therapeutic relationship. The therapeutic relationship has great influence on therapeutic adherence and success. Many factors influence the therapeutic relationship and they include the practitioner psychologist's own attachment style, lived experience of mental health problems and attitude to self disclosure.

The therapeutic relationship

According to Bordin (1979), the therapeutic relationship is based on the following:

- Agreement on therapeutic goals.
- Agreement on the tasks necessary to achieve those goals.
- The development of a personal alliance between therapist and service user.

Attachment

With a focus on the therapeutic alliance, as illustrated in the cycle of caring, we need to consider the unique profile of the practitioner psychologist in terms of their relationship style and how this influences the development of a relationship with the service user. It is true that with good training and experience, our own personality or unique attributes should not interfere with the development of a therapeutic relationship. However, the experience of developing that therapeutic relationship time and time again will take a toll on some individuals more than others. The nature of our attachment style is a key factor in whether a therapeutic relationship becomes an additional or significant stressor.

Bowlby (1969) introduced the idea of attachment based on parent–infant relationships formed after birth. Infants need to feel secure so that they can explore the world knowing they have a safe, secure place to return to should the world become frightening or uninteresting. With careful caregiving, an infant develops a secure attachment style with their caregivers, in which they learn to trust themselves and others. If caregiving is insufficient, it can result in weaker bonds of attachment, and affect the infant's ability to form trusting and secure relationships. Ainsworth, Blehar, Waters and Wall (1978) categorised these early relationships as secure, anxious/ambivalent and avoidant. Ainsworth and colleagues theorised that children who have secure attachments have more cooperative relationships with adults, are more sociable and popular with peers, and have more reliable relationships. Hazan and Shaver (1990) adapted Bowlby's theory to adult work environments. They argue that the work environment elicits 'exploration' behaviour. Hazan and Shaver matched the following behaviours in work environments with the three attachment styles:

- Secure – the individual has a positive approach to work, is least likely to put off work, to feel failure and rejection, and is likely to feel safe in the work environment.
- Anxious/ambivalent – the individual prefers to work with others, is likely to feel misunderstood and under-appreciated, is motivated by approval, and is likely to worry that their work will lead to others rejecting them.
- Avoidant – the individual may feel nervous when they are not working and may therefore overwork, allowing their professional life to interfere with their personal life and health (leaving little room to spend time with others). Crucially, individuals with this type of attachment style tend to use work as a reason to avoiding forming relationships with others.

Leiper and Casares (2000) explored the attachment styles of 196 practising Clinical Psychologists in the UK. Their interest was not only in the psychologists' attachment style, but in how this related to the challenges and rewards they experienced in their practice, and their levels of satisfaction, support and felt competence in their work. Although a large majority of the sample rated their attachment as secure, 27.6% rated themselves as insecure. Those who described themselves as insecure were either avoidant (18.4%) or anxious/

ambivalent (9.2%). Participants who rated themselves as insecure scored higher on measures for self-reliance, angry withdrawal, early life loss events and parental response that lacked empathy. Importantly, the study found a significant difference between the secure and insecure group on their approaches to work. Therapists who rated themselves as insecure were more likely to have difficulty in therapeutic practice, blame themselves for these difficulties, experience less reward, perceive lower levels of support at work, and experience difficulties in maintaining a balance between their work and personal life. These results accord with Hazan and Shaver's (1990) findings with the general adult population.

The nature of attachment among practitioner psychologists is therefore key in how they approach their work and, more importantly, relate to others, both service users and work colleagues. For example, if an avoidant individual avoids close relationships in the work environment, the question that needs to be asked is: 'In what way does this impact on the quality of the therapeutic alliance?' Based on the Leiper and Casares (2000) study, it is clear that practitioner psychologists are not driven primarily to choose this particular career based on their individual attachment style. It is also true that individuals cannot be put into discrete categories. However, being self-aware, exploring your own relationship style and considering how it might impact on your therapeutic work might help you to build resilience in your day-to-day practice. Considering the relationship style of the service user and how this interacts with the practitioner's relationship style will also be useful. Such issues could usefully be discussed in supervision.

Mental health

I often ask my Master's students the question: 'Can someone who themselves experiences or has experienced mental health problems become a practitioner psychologist?' Thankfully the majority respond positively and state that if the psychologist practises good self-care and manages their symptoms adequately, there is nothing to stop them becoming a practitioner psychologist. Why question this, though? You may be aware that many of those working in the mental health field have had their own mental health problems or care for others who have mental health problems. Much of this experience drives the individual to pursue a career in the field due to their own psychological wounds and difficult experiences (Barnett et al., 2007). It is also true that an established practitioner psychologist may develop mental health problems during the course of their career. Indeed, the practitioner psychologist is just as susceptible to mental health problems or other difficulties, such as substance abuse, chronic illness, relationship problems, bereavement, etc., and despite the prevailing idea that the psychologist's training somehow protects them from these difficulties, it is more likely that they are at greater risk than the general population (Sherman, 1998).

Despite the response from my Master's students, the fact remains that those in the mental health professions may see their own difficulties as a sign of weakness and feel shame and fear of being judged by others, as well as fearing that their career prospects may be negatively affected (Corrigan, 2004; Garelick, 2012). This in turn may mean that they do not seek the help they need or even recognise the signs that their mental health is deteriorating. In an anonymous, online study by Tay, Alcock and Scior (2018), responses were collected from 678 UK Clinical Psychologists. Over half of the participants disclosed that they had experienced a mental health problem at some point during their lives (62.7%), with almost half that figure experiencing more than one mental health problem. The most commonly reported mental health problems were depression and anxiety, with a small number experiencing bipolar disorder (1.2%), substance addiction (4.2%), an eating disorder (11.1%) or psychosis (3.3%). These figures exceed estimates from the Mental Health Foundation (2016) that there is a 41% prevalence for mental health problems among the general adult population in the UK. Some participants in the study by Tay and colleagues (2017) had not disclosed their mental health problem (10.8%), stating that they feared negative judgement. These are sobering statistics, and suggest that interventions aimed at helping practitioners in the health and social care sector would serve the dual purpose of acknowledging the presence of these difficulties and encouraging practitioner psychologists (and indeed others who work in health and social care) to seek help.

What is often overlooked in research on the mental health of practitioners is the potential benefit of lived experience (Tay et al., 2017). This is not to say that a practitioner psychologist should have lived experience in order to fully understand another's struggles with mental health. It could be argued that lived experience may present a certain bias, which needs to be addressed reflectively. That said, there are those who argue that lived experience can benefit the therapeutic alliance, through self-disclosure. This is highly controversial (Henretty, Currier, Berman, & Levitt, 2014) and not everyone agrees that self-disclosure benefits the therapeutic relationship. To overcome life events makes us human, but the sharing of those struggles may indicate that we have not overcome them or have accepted the impact of those challenges, or that those struggles and challenges persist and indicate that there is more work to be done.

Self-disclosure

Self-disclosure is the practitioner sharing something personal with the service user (Hill & Knox, 2001) and such disclosures can be 'facts, feelings, insight, strategies, reassurance/support, challenge, and immediacy' (Knox & Hill, 2003: 530). The use of self-disclosure can be informed by theoretical orientation. A humanistic approach encourages therapist self-disclosure as it implies genuineness and positive regard (Robitschek & McCarthy, 1991), and the cognitive behavioural tradition regards self-disclosure as useful in strengthening the therapeutic relationship, normalising experiences and challenging negative interpretations. There does, however, need to be deliberate exploration of the intentions of using self-disclosure as part of an intervention or therapeutic orientation. As noted by Audet (2011), therapist disclosure may lead to the crossing of boundaries, reduce the service user's perception of the practitioner's credibility and competence, and can compromise how the service user perceives their role and the role of the therapist. In contrast, Audet also shows that perceptions of credibility and competence can be increased and there can be better recognition of roles within the therapeutic relationship.

Although there are many forms and types of self-disclosure, what we are discussing here is the disclosure which reveals information about the therapist's life and experiences. This type of disclosure can establish rapport and show that the therapist is also human and subject to the same life issues that can befall everyone. When a practitioner psychologist identifies with the service user's struggles, there is a greater likelihood of self-disclosure. It is this identification and the self-awareness required in order to understand the nature of this identification that should be focused on. There can be unawareness of inner struggles that only become apparent when a service user discloses something that triggers an emotional response, or there may be unawareness of the influence of past or current struggles on therapeutic work. To protect the therapist and service user, reflecting upon such occurrences is essential.

You may be confident that you would only use self-disclosure where necessary, or maybe you do not wish to self-disclose at all. However, as practitioner psychologists, you may be working with colleagues or be supervising others who wish to or have used self-disclosure. As a supervisor, it is your responsibility to ensure that the supervisee is competent in their therapeutic work and that they understand the rationale behind self-disclosure and what is best practice regarding self-disclosure. Henretty and Levitt (2010) conducted an extensive review of the literature on the topic of self-disclosure and provide a list of dos and don'ts that you might find useful in your own work.

Self-disclosure

According to Henretty and Levitt (2010), do use self-disclosure:

- To foster the therapeutic alliance
- To model alternative behaviours and perceptions to service users
- To encourage service user autonomy
- To encourage self-exploration

- To normalise
- To equalise power.

Do not use self-disclosure:

- To control or manipulate
- To reassure service users when it is not therapeutically appropriate to do so
- To display passive aggression
- To emphasise power differences/dissimilarities
- To seek validation/approval
- To express emotion
- To inadvertently blur boundaries.

As a practitioner psychologist, the challenges that arise within the work organisation and the therapeutic relationship and around attachment, mental health and self-disclosure can lead to compassion fatigue, vicarious trauma and burnout (see Figure 9.1).

Compassion Fatigue

The cumulative effects of working with survivors of trauma or perpetrators of abuse on a day-to-day basis can lead to compassion fatigue, when the practitioner becomes so emotionally and physically exhausted that they find it harder to maintain empathy and compassion for the service user. It is important to note that compassion fatigue is not an immediate effect, as notable in secondary and vicarious trauma (Newell & MacNeil, 2010). While over-exposure to human suffering can lead to lowered compassion towards service users, it can also impact other areas of the practitioner psychologist's life (Geoffrion, Morselli, & Guay, 2016). For example, exposure to service users' trauma may

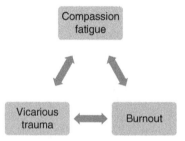

Figure 9.1   The impacts of caring

trigger the practitioner psychologist's own history of trauma, with the result that compassion fatigue can lead to doubts about professional competence and the practitioner's sense of self.

Compassion fatigue

Geoffrion et al. (2016) and Merriman (2015) list the specific emotional, behavioural and cognitive signs of compassion fatigue:

- Difficulties in sleeping
- Increased reactivity to stress
- Avoidance
- Intrusive thoughts about work activity
- A lower capacity for intimacy
- The blurring of boundaries between work and home
- A loss of purpose and confidence
- An increase in self-soothing behaviours
- Dread of working with service users
- Anxiety and depression.

Risk factors for compassion fatigue include large caseloads, caseloads that mainly include service users who have experienced severe trauma and abuse, and a lack of support and resources (Skovholt & Trotter-Mathison, 2016). Protective factors to mitigate the potential for compassion fatigue include effective supervision, organisational support in creating positive work practices and an organisational focus on personal wellness.

Vicarious Trauma

Vicarious trauma has been defined as 'a long-term alteration in the therapist's own cognitive schemas, or beliefs, expectations, and assumptions about the self and others' (McCann & Pearlman, 1990: 132). It arises as a consequence of over-exposure to service users' stories of suffering and hardship. McCann and Pearlman, the originators of the term, state that a change in cognitive schema can make the psychologist lose their trust in others, increase their vulnerability, increase their feelings of powerlessness and pessimism, and lead to their alienation or separateness from others. Vicarious trauma is included in the fifth edition of the *Diagnostic and Statistical Manual of Mental Disorders* (DSM-5; American Psychiatric Association, 2013), which describes vicarious trauma as resulting from repeated exposure to trauma stories in a professional role, leading to post-traumatic stress disorder (PTSD).

Burnout

Burnout is a state of emotional, physical and mental exhaustion as a result of exposure to excessive and prolonged stress. Di Benedetto and Swadling (2014) suggest that the sources of burnout can be personal, work-related or service user-related. In this section we will focus on work-related burnout. According to Kahill (1986), the term 'burnout' was first introduced by Freudenberger, who described burnout as 'to fail, wear out, or become exhausted by making excessive demands on energy, strength, or resources' (Freudenberger, 1974: 1043). Maslach, Schaufeli and Leiter (2001) conceptualise work-related burnout as a psychological response to ongoing interpersonal stressors caused by the work.

Work-related burnout

Three key dimensions of work-related burnout (Maslach et al., 2001) are:

- Overwhelming exhaustion – being over-extended beyond individual emotional and physical resources.
- Cynicism – being detached from various aspects of the job.
- Reduced efficacy – feelings of incompetence and inadequate accomplishment and achievement.

What causes burnout?

Many theories have been postulated with regard to what causes burnout. Vredenburgh, Carlozzi and Stein (1999) found that in their sample of Counselling Psychologists, the work setting was a significant factor in contributing to variances in personal accomplishment and the depersonalisation of service users. In Vredenburgh et al.'s study, Counselling Psychologists in private practice had lower levels of burnout, suggesting that settings where there were fewer organisational demands and where practitioners had more autonomy were less stressful. This finding supports the factors outlined by Di Benedetto and Swadling (2014), who found that heavy workload and early-career positions, where practitioners were reliant on more experienced colleagues for guidance and supervision, were notable factors in the development of burnout. Both factors reduce autonomy, with organisational demands governing workload and early-career practitioners being reliant on more experienced colleagues for guidance and supervision.

Signs indicating burnout

Behaviours that might indicate burnout (Barnett et al., 2007; Di Benedetto & Swadling, 2014) include:

- Discussing work frustrations with colleagues and friends
- Avoiding thinking of service users outside work
- Engaging in personal therapy
- Using substances to relax
- Displaying increased frustration or anger towards service users
- Experiencing greater stress within personal lives
- Showing signs of boredom and fatigue
- Hoping that service users will cancel
- Finding less enjoyment in the work environment.

Stress

Stress is what enables us to function. One of the most important stress hormones, cortisol, is what gets us up in the morning. However, too much stress over time can have negative consequences. The transactional model of stress (Folkman & Lazarus, 1984) asserts that the impact of a perceived stressor on an individual is a result of a number of factors. First, the individual has to determine that an event or other potential stressor is in fact a stressor. The subsequent impact of the stressor can then be mitigated by coping style, which, in turn, is mediated by an environment providing social support. Therefore, stress is only a problem when the demands outweigh resources.

There is a responsibility on the practitioner to recognise signs of chronic stress in the workplace and to mitigate these factors as much as possible. This is not easy, especially as the practitioner psychologist is trained to meet the needs of others and can therefore fail to recognise their own needs. Crucially, there is a risk it can lead to impaired competence (Barnett et al., 2007). The practitioner psychologist needs to be aware of the work environment, and of themselves, in order to monitor areas of concern.

According to Rabin, Feldman and Kaplan (1999), we need to consider two areas when considering self-care. Rabin and colleagues assert that the focus should be on prevention of stress, and stress management.

Preventing the impact of stress

A multidimensional approach to preventing stress is described by Maslach and Goldberg (1998), who focus specifically on burnout. They target three areas of burnout: (1) emotional exhaustion, (2) depersonalisation, and (3) a sense of accomplishment. The benefit of the approach is that its effectiveness can be more easily measured.

Kramen-Kahn and Hansen (1998) encourage a balance between work and personal life as the best way to prevent stress. They suggest that ensuring diversity in work practices, maintaining a diverse caseload, taking regular work breaks, getting plenty of rest and taking regular exercise contribute to building resilience to stress. A focus on our social, psychological and physiological needs should not be regarded as an unnecessary luxury; to mitigate stress and to ensure the best care for service users, practitioner psychologists need to engage in positive self-care practices for themselves.

Self-care Strategies

The self-care strategies listed here are from *The Resilient Practitioner* (Skovholt & Trotter-Mathison, 2016). It is one of the most comprehensive texts on the topic of resilience for professionals working in the health and social care services. Skovholt and Trotter-Mathison include many reflective exercises that will be useful in helping you to develop your own self-awareness. Their self-care strategies include the following:

1. Spending time with family (to ensure a good work–life balance).
2. Undertaking continuing professional development.
3. Partaking in hobbies that are fun.
4. Taking regular exercise.
5. Reading.
6. Undertaking regular supervision.
7. Maintaining social connections.
8. Making time for self.
9. Taking regular holidays.

Self-care is also important in day-to-day work tasks, and there are things you can do to manage your work. Balance your diary and don't see too many service users in one day, as you need some time to prepare and to de-stress before and after each service user. Be mindful of your emotional state throughout the day; check in with how you are feeling in that moment, without judgement. Use breathing exercises to maintain your emotional state and ground yourself in the 'here and now'. Laugh with colleagues, take a lunch break, clear your desk. It is not a luxury to practise self-care, but a necessity not only for your own wellbeing, but also for that of the service user.

Vicarious resilience

When faced with service users who have experienced immeasurable trauma, it is surprising to consider that there can be beneficial effects from this type of work. Termed 'vicarious resilience', it is defined as 'a unique and positive effect that transforms therapists in response to service user trauma survivors' own resiliency' (Hernández, Gangsei, & Engstrom, 2007: 237). Resilience is the ability to 'bounce back' from adversity and in therapy can occur in three areas: (1) self-perception, (2) relationships, and (3) philosophy (Arnold, Calhoun, Tedeschi & Cann, 2005). Hernández, Engstrom and Gangsei (2010) list the following factors as leading to resilient growth:

1. Witnessing service users' capacity to heal.
2. Recognising the value of therapy.
3. Hope.
4. Reassessing one's own problems.
5. Spiritual healing.

Vicarious resilience is a common occurrence in trauma work, and is more likely to occur where there is therapeutic attunement and conscious attention (Hernández et al., 2007).

Summary

A great deal of this chapter may appear to be devoted to the negative elements of working as a practitioner psychologist. However, my aim is to truly capture the realities of working in the mental health field and for the reader to recognise that, despite their motivation to 'help others', it is not enough to carry you through a career as a practitioner psychologist. The practitioner needs to be aware of the 'why' they chose a career as a practitioner psychologist. If it is based on personal experience of mental health (either own or another's), then the practitioner needs to be wary of how it may impact on their work. Alternatively, the practitioner may be driven by a keen interest in psychological theory and mental health.

The aim of this chapter was to highlight areas where practitioner resilience may be tested and where it may flourish. Self-awareness is key, and the reader should explore the reasons for their choice of career. There is no 'wrong' reason, but to understand their motivation is to better prepare. There are unique challenges to the work of a psychologist and the emotional demands of working with service users generally, when their situation does not improve, and administrative and organisational tasks can be exhausting.

Attuning to service users and experiencing their feelings as our own can be exhausting or exhilarating. The cycle of caring involves empathic attachment, active involvement and felt separation, which are experienced time and time again with each service user. The ability to deal with this is a professional skill, and should be developed in the same way as any other skill required of the profession. Areas of potential challenge can be organisational or personal, such as practitioner mental health, and process-related, such as the therapeutic relationship. Attachment is a key feature in this chapter and is something that is often missed when the therapeutic alliance is discussed in the literature. Not only is the attachment behaviour of the practitioner an important factor, but so is the attachment of the service user. It is not advised to explore attachment styles in-session, but recognising attachment styles may guide reflection or supervision.

The chapter has also covered more serious outcomes, such as compassion fatigue, vicarious trauma and burnout. It is important that you are aware of these potential outcomes and engage in your own self-care.

Key Points

- Working as a practitioner psychologist is a challenging but rewarding career path that leads to lifelong learning and the many rewards of helping others.
- Practitioners are at risk of developing or experiencing life challenges, struggles and mental health problems as much as service users.
- Supervision, reflective practice, leadership and multidisciplinary team working are key skills in supporting practitioner resilience.
- Although periods of difficulty may occur, it is possible to grow as a result of these and develop greater resilience.
- As in any profession, self-care is a priority; it is not a luxury, but a necessity.

Practice Case Studies

Case Study 1

You are working in a residential forensic setting as a Clinical Psychologist. You enjoy your work and have a good relationship with colleagues. You have worked in this role for 10 years and feel confident but sometimes unfulfilled. You have a young family, a hefty mortgage and find yourself using the comfort of your workplace as an escape. Changing your job now does not feel possible.

You have supervision on a monthly basis and enjoy chatting to your supervisor about the therapeutic work that you're undertaking with your allocated service users. The supervisor is an old friend and you tend to spend a lot of the time chatting about your respective families. You've settled into a routine that involves using tried-and-tested therapies and group work, and despite the odd training day, your therapeutic methods remain the same as they were when you started in the role.

Your dissatisfaction with the role you're in and lack of accomplishment is being triggered by a new colleague who is younger than you, newly qualified and full of ideas. They keep asking for your advice and you realise that you do not have much to give that is up to date and that does not sound like you've not changed your practice in many years. You have begun to dread seeing your colleague and work doesn't feel like much of a sanctuary anymore.

Suggested questions

1. What can you do to improve this situation? What areas can you focus on?
2. If nothing changes, what could the potential outcomes be?

Case Study 2

You have recently qualified as a Counselling Psychologist and have started work in a family therapy unit. You often feel that you don't belong in your role and put this down to 'imposter syndrome' and the fact that you are newly qualified. You are passionate about the work, though, and having had a difficult time as a young child with your own family, you are determined to help other families avoid the trauma you experienced.

A recent addition to your caseload is a couple who have a 5-year-old child. The child has demonstrated significant behavioural difficulties and is due to be assessed for attention deficit disorder. The couple have a difficult relationship and you feel that their arguments are significantly impacting on the child. In fact, you identify a great deal with the child and find yourself leaving your sessions with the couple an emotional wreck.

You have begun to dread seeing this couple and hope that they cancel their session. You find yourself becoming distracted and you have been unable to talk about this with your supervisor as you feel it will make them think that you can't do this job. Outside work you tend to keep to yourself, and don't socialise much. You have had a couple of short-term relationships, but these tend to cause you more stress, which you feel you don't need at this time. You are quite happy to rush home from work and to open that bottle of wine.

Suggested questions

1. What are the risk factors in the case study that may lead to burnout?
2. What could you do to better support yourself?

References

Ainsworth, M. D. S., Blehar, M., Waters, E., & Wall, S. (1978). *Patterns of Attachment: A Psychological Study of the Strange Situation*. Mahwah, NJ: Lawrence Erlbaum.

American Psychiatric Association. (2013). *Diagnostic and Statistical Manual of Mental Disorders, Fifth Edition* (DSM-5). Washington, DC: APA.

Arnold, D., Calhoun, L. G., Tedeschi, R., & Cann, A. (2005). Vicarious posttraumatic growth in psychotherapy. *Journal of Humanistic Psychology, 45*(2), 239–263.

Audet, C. T. (2011). Service user perspectives of therapist self-disclosure: Violating boundaries or removing barriers? *Counselling Psychology Quarterly, 24*(2), 85–100.

Barnett, J. E., Baker, E. K., Elman, N. S., & Schoener, G. R. (2007). In pursuit of wellness: The self-care imperative. *Professional Psychology: Research and Practice, 38*(6), 603a.

Bordin, E. (1979). The generalizability for the psychoanalytic concept of the working alliance. *Psychotherapy: Theory, Research and Practice, 16*, 252–260.

Bowlby, J. (1969). *Attachment and Loss v. 3* (Vol. 1). New York: Random House.

Corrigan, P. (2004). How stigma interferes with mental health care. *American Psychologist, 59*(7), 614.

Di Benedetto, M., & Swadling, M. (2014). Burnout in Australian psychologists: Correlations with work-setting, mindfulness and self-care behaviours. *Psychology, Health & Medicine, 19*(6), 705–715.

Folkman, S., & Lazarus, R. S. (1984). *Stress, Appraisal, and Coping*. New York: Springer.

Freudenberger, H. J. (1974). Staff burnout. *Journal of Social Issues, 30*(1), 159–165.

Garelick, A. I. (2012). Doctors' health: Stigma and the professional discomfort in seeking help. *The Psychiatrist, 36*(3), 81–84.

Geoffrion, S., Morselli, C., & Guay, S. (2016). Rethinking compassion fatigue through the lens of professional identity: The case of child-protection workers. *Trauma, Violence, & Abuse, 17*(3), 270–283.

Hazan, C., & Shaver, P. R. (1990). Love and work: An attachment-theoretical perspective. *Journal of Personality and Social Psychology, 59*(2), 270.

Henretty, J. R., Currier, J. M., Berman, J. S., & Levitt, H. M. (2014). The impact of counselor self-disclosure on service users: A meta-analytic review of experimental and quasi-experimental research. *Journal of Counseling Psychology, 61*(2), 191–207. https://doi.org/10.1037/a0036189

Henretty, J. R., & Levitt, H. M. (2010). The role of therapist self-disclosure in psychotherapy: A qualitative review. *Clinical Psychology Review, 30*(1), 63–77.

Hernández, P., Engstrom, D., & Gangsei, D. (2010). Exploring the impact of trauma on therapists: Vicarious resilience and related concepts in training. *Journal of Systemic Therapies, 29*(1), 67–83.

Hernández, P., Gangsei, D., & Engstrom, D. (2007). Vicarious resilience: A new concept in work with those who survive trauma. *Family Process, 46*(2), 229–241.

Hill, C. E., & Knox, S. (2001). Self-disclosure. *Psychotherapy: Theory, Research, Practice, Training, 38*(4), 413.

Kahill, S. (1986). Relationship of burnout among professional psychologists to professional expectations and social support. *Psychological Reports, 59*(3), 1043–1051.

Knox, S., & Hill, C. E. (2003). Therapist self-disclosure: Research-based suggestions for practitioners. *Journal of Clinical Psychology, 59*(5), 529–539.

Kramen-Kahn, B., & Hansen, N. D. (1998). Rafting the rapids: Occupational hazards, rewards, and coping strategies of psychotherapists. *Professional Psychology: Research and Practice, 29*(2), 130.

Leiper, R., & Casares, P. (2000). An investigation of the attachment organization of clinical psychologists and its relationship to clinical practice. *British Journal of Medical Psychology, 73*(4), 449–464.

Maslach, C., & Goldberg, J. (1998). Prevention of burnout: New perspectives. *Applied and Preventive Psychology, 7*(1), 63–74.

Maslach, C., Schaufeli, W. B., & Leiter, M. P. (2001). Job burnout. *Annual Review of Psychology, 52*(1), 397–422.

McCann, I. L., & Pearlman, L. A. (1990). Vicarious traumatization: A framework for understanding the psychological effects of working with victims. *Journal of Traumatic Stress, 3*(1), 131–149.

Mental Health Foundation. (2016). *Fundamental Facts about Mental Health 2016.* London: Mental Health Foundation. Retrieved from www.mentalhealth.org.uk/publi cations/fundamental-facts-about-mental-health-2016

Merriman, J. (2015). Enhancing counselor supervision through compassion fatigue education. *Journal of Counseling & Development, 93*(3), 370–378.

Newell, J. M., & MacNeil, G. A. (2010). Professional burnout, vicarious trauma, secondary traumatic stress, and compassion fatigue. *Best Practices in Mental Health, 6*(2), 57–68.

Rabin, S., Feldman, D., & Kaplan, Z. E. (1999). Stress and intervention strategies in mental health professionals. *British Journal of Medical Psychology, 72*(2), 159–169.

Robitschek, C. G., & McCarthy, P. R. (1991). Prevalence of counselor self-reference in the therapeutic dyad. *Journal of Counseling & Development, 69*(3), 218–221.

Sherman, J. J. (1998). Effects of psychotherapeutic treatments for PTSD: A meta-analysis of controlled clinical trials. *Journal of Traumatic Stress: Official Publication of the International Society for Traumatic Stress Studies, 11*(3), 413–435.

Skovholt, T. M. (2005). The cycle of caring: A model of expertise in the helping professions. *Journal of Mental Health Counseling, 27*(1), 82–93.

Skovholt, T. M., & Trotter-Mathison, M. (2016). *The Resilient Practitioner: Burnout and Compassion Fatigue Prevention and Self-care Strategies for the Helping Professions.* Abingdon: Routledge.

Tay, S., Alcock, K., & Scior, K. (2018). Mental health problems among clinical psychologists: Stigma and its impact on disclosure and help-seeking. *Journal of Clinical Psychology, 74*(9), 1545–1555.

Vredenburgh, L. D., Carlozzi, A. F., & Stein, L. B. (1999). Burnout in counseling psychologists: Type of practice setting and pertinent demographics. *Counselling Psychology Quarterly, 12*(3), 293–302.

Yalom, I. D. (2002). *The Gift of Therapy: An Open Letter to a New Generation of Therapists and Their Patients.* New York: HarperCollins.

Index

clinical neuropsychology, xx
clinical psychologists, xviii–xix, 102–4, 136,
    148–9, 150
Clinical Psychology Leadership Development
    Framework, 136, 137, 138
clinical supervision
    Bernard's discrimination model, 46–7
    British Psychological Society, 40–1, 46–7
    case studies, 51–2
    challenges in, 47–8
    cognitive behavioural modality, 43–4
    and competence, 40
    confidentiality, 60
    contracts, 40–2
    discrimination, 97
    effective supervisors, 42–3
    ethics, 38–9, 40, 58–9
    integrative models of supervision, 45–7
    leadership, 130, 134
    models, 44–7
    multicultural aspects of, 49–50
    notes, 39, 41
    overview, 37–8, 50–1
    person-centred modality, 44
    psychodynamic modality, 43
    reflective practice, 38, 41, 124
    Ronnestad and Skovholt's
        development model, 46
    self-disclosure, 151
    self-leadership, 139
    and service users, 39
    solution-focused modality, 44
Cochrane, 7, 12
Code of Ethics and Conduct, 40, 58, 59
Code of Human Research Ethics, 56, 57, 65–6,
    68, 69
cognitive analytic therapy, 16
cognitive behavioural therapy, 13, 14, 17, 43–4, 151
Coleman, G., 102
communication, 11, 15, 25–6, 87
comparator test, 96
compassion fatigue, 146, 152–3, 158
competence, 40, 48, 58, 59, 69
confidentiality, 47, 59–61, 62, 64, 69, 70, 75, 119
conflict, 26–8
consent, 39, 50, 60, 63–5, 66–8, 69, 76, 119–20
consultees, 67
contingency theories, 131–3
contingent reinforcement, 132
continuing professional development, 8, 15,
    29, 38, 41, 136, 139
conversion courses, xvi–xvii
Corrigan, P.W., 137, 138
cortisol, 155
counselling, xxii
counselling psychologists, xix, 154
Court, A.J., 8
Crawford, M., 63
Criminal Justice and Court Service Act (2000), 75

critical analysis, 117, 120
critical reflection, 113, 117–27, 136
cultural competence, 49, 105
culture, 28–9, 104, 105, 118
cycle of caring, 146, 147, 158
Cyert, R.M., 129

Data Protection Act (2018), 61–2
databases, evidence-based, 6–7
Delworth, U., 45
depression, 14, 150, 153
Despenser, S., 80–1
Dewey, J., 113–14, 115, 116
Di Benedetto, M., 154
*Diagnostic and Statistical Manual of Mental
    Disorders*, 153
dialectical behaviour therapy, 16
direct discrimination, 94–5
disability, 94, 95, 102, 103tab
Disability Discrimination Act (1995), 94
discrimination
    case studies, 108–9
    clinical supervision, 97
    direct and indirect, 94–6
    interpersonal, 97–101
    legal perspective, 94–6
    micro-agressions, 98–100
    organisational, 101–4
    against practitioner psychologists, 101
    practitioner psychologists against, 106–7
    professional guidelines on, 107
    reflective practice, 97
    societal, 104–5
    training against, 105–6, 107
    see also anti-discriminatory practice;
        Equality Act (2010)
diversity, 49, 50, 97, 98, 100, 102–4, 105, 107
Division of Neuropsychology (DoN), xxi
Doctorates, xvii, xix, xx, xxi
double-blind studies, 5

education, 105–7
educational psychologists, xx, xxi
effectiveness, 4, 6, 12, 14, 15, 16
efficacy, 4, 6, 14, 15, 16
Egdell case, 60
Ehrhart, M.G., 135–6
empirically supported treatments, 2, 3, 4fig, 8,
    12–14, 15
*English Survey of Applied Psychologists in
    Health and Social Care*, 102
Equality Act (2010), 93–6, 100, 101
*The Equality Act 2010 in Mental Health: A
    Guide to Implementation and Issues for
    Practice*, 93
equality duty, 96
equality training, 107
ethics
    boundaries, 57–8, 70

scaffolding, 45
Scaratti, G., 30
Schmitt, M.T., 101
Schön, D.A., 114–15, 116, 117
schools, 33–4
science, 59, 115
scientist-practitioners, xiii, xviii, 2–3, 13, 16,
    59, 106, 107
Scottish Intercollegiate Guidelines Network
    (SIGN), 7
secure attachment style, 148–9
self-awareness, 120–1, 122, 123, 125, 130, 135,
    136, 151, 157
self-care, 149, 156, 158
self-disclosure, 42, 48, 58, 119, 147, 150–2
self-harm, 16, 33–4, 60, 66, 80, 81–3, 146
*Self-harm, Suicide and Risk: Helping People
    who Self-harm*, 81
self-leadership, 139–40, 141
self-neglect, 83–4
service users, 3, 4fig, 8, 10–12, 13, 14, 15, 16,
    39
Sex Discrimination Act (1975), 94
sexual orientation, 50, 85, 94, 99, 102, 103tab,
    105
Sharma, M.K., 137, 138
Shaver, P.R., 148, 149
SIS: Suicidal Intent Scale, 79tab
Skovholt, T.M., 146, 156
Slattery, J.M., 57
Smith, E., 117–19, 123
Smith, P., 125
societal discrimination, 98fig, 104–5
solution-focused modality, 44
Sonne, J.L., 57
Sosik, J.J., 134, 135
Spalding, E., 122
sports psychologists, xxi
Spring, B., 3, 4fig, 10
standards, 56, 57
*Standards of Conduct, Performance and
    Ethics*, 58, 97, 100
*Standards of Proficiency for Practitioner
    Psychologists*, 58
Starbucks, 106
Static-2002R, 78tab
stereotyping, 99, 104
Stirman, S.W., 14
Stoltenberg, C., 45
stress, 28, 29, 147, 153, 154, 155–6
students, 119–20
substance abuse, 80, 86, 149, 150
Sue, D.W., 99
suicide, 60, 81–3, 146

supervision *see* clinical supervision
Sutton, L., 121–2
Swadling, M., 154
systematic reviews, 4, 5, 7
Szmukler, G., 87

Tay, S., 150
team climate, 137, 138
technical eclecticism, 46
theoretical integration, 46
therapeutic modalities, 43–4
therapeutic relationship, 147, 148, 151,
    152, 158
Thomas, J.T., 40, 49
three-legged stool model, 3, 4fig
Tolin, D.F., 12–13
training, xvii, 105–7
transactional leadership, 132, 133, 141
transactional model, stress, 155
transformational leadership, 132, 133, 134,
    140, 141
transitions, 83
trauma, 146, 152–3, 157
Tribe, R., 60, 105
Trotter-Mathison, M., 146, 156
Tuckman, B.W., 23, 24
Turpin, G., 102

UK Council for Psychotherapy (UKCP), xxii
unconscious bias, 106

values, 3, 4fig, 10–12, 13, 14, 15, 16, 31, 57,
    58, 63, 117, 130, 131, 132, 136, 147
Varshney, M., 80
Vasquez, M.J., 59
vicarious resilience, 157
vicarious trauma, 152fig, 153, 158
victimisation, 96
violence, 66, 76, 80–1
volunteering, xviii, xxii
VRAG: Violence Risk Appraisal Guide, 79tab
Vredenburgh, L.D., 154

Webster-Wright, A., 121
What Makes a Good Capacity Assessment,
    64, 65
whistleblownig, 48
Woodbridge, B., 10
Woods, P., 77
Woolf, S.H., 8
work experience, xxii–xxiii

Yoho, S.K., 139
young people, 61, 83